American Hist
SIMULATIONS

Written by Max W. Fischer

Illustrated by Blanca Apodaca

Mrs. Whitaker

Teacher Created Materials, Inc.
P.O. Box 1040
Huntington Beach, CA 92647
©1993 Teacher Created Materials, Inc.
Made in U.S.A.

ISBN 1-55734-480-9

Table of Contents

Introduction 3

Success with Simulations 4

Cooperative Learning Teams 5

Simulations

   1 — Artifact Inquiry (Archaeology) 6
   2 — ''Odd Man Out'' Trade Review (Age of Discovery) 8
   3 — Brown Gold (New World Exploration) 14
   4 — Treasure Map (New World Exploration) 17
   5 — Coronado's Telephone (New World Exploration) 21
   6 — Blind Passage (Northwest Passage) 24
   7 — A Question of Tolerance (Puritans) 27
   8 — Reprieve Granted (Settlement of Georgia Colony) 31
   9 — The King's M & M's® (The Stamp Act) 34
  10 — I Spy (Revolutionary War) 40
  11 — Consensus (Articles of Confederation) 43
  12 — Land Grab (Northwest Ordinance) 45
  13 — Compromise (Constitution) 49
  14 — Widget Assembly (Industrial Revolution) 51
  15 — Hands Off! (The Monroe Doctrine) 55
  16 — The Heartbreak of Pioneering (Westward Settlement) . . . 58
  17 — Move Out! (Immigrants/Forced Removal of Indians) 61
  18 — Merchants and Miners (California Gold Rush) 64
  19 — A Classroom Divided (The Civil War) 69
  20 — Sanctuary (Underground Railroad/Current Events) 71
  21 — Rockefeller (Rise of Industrialism) 74
  22 — How the West Was Won (Indian Wars of the West) 77
  23 — Jim Crow (Segregation) 79
  24 — Muckraker's Cake (Progressive Reform in the early 1900's) . . . 81
  25 — A Woman's Place . . . (Women's Suffrage Movement) . . . 83
  26 — Crash (Stock Market Collapse of 1929) 85
  27 — Does the Buck Stop Here? (Watergate) 89

Management Tools

Simulation Savvy Certificate 92
Awards and Rewards 93
United States Map 94
World Map 95
Brainstorming Web 96

Introduction

History would be so fascinating if one could only relive it. In technology's never-ending march, man's innovation may someday perfect time travel so that students could learn directly from the past. Until such a time, we will need to rely on the innovative tools of the present. Simulations provide one way in which we can bring the past into the present.

The ninety-six pages of *American History Simulations* are filled with activities designed to involve students affectively as they study the events of United States history. Simulations, problem-solving dilemmas, and review of material through game simulations excite students to want to learn about the causes and implications of events which often changed the course of American history and which affect us today.

Many of the activities place students in the middle of a situation relevant to a famous episode in history. Students do get involved!

The activities in *American History Simulations* may be used as anticipatory sets for an upcoming lesson or unit. Some simulation activities can be used to bring closure to a lesson already covered. Encompassing cooperative learning, many of the activities stress critical thinking skills and/or cognitive review of text-based material.

American History Simulations has been developed as a supplement to the classroom textbook and curriculum requirements. Most of the activities can be completed within thirty minutes. A few simulations are organized to specifically accompany an entire ongoing chapter on a particular period of history, such as the Civil War.

The simulations are presented in chronological order and easily accompany the history text. In addition, each activity is structured in an easy-to-follow lesson plan format that teachers will appreciate.

Success With Simulations

The activities in *American History Simulations* have been selected in order to get students affectively involved with history by simulating conditions of a particular historical era within the limited confines of the school environment.

Whether you intend to use a simulation for the purposes of introduction, review, or as part of the closure process, establish procedures throughout each unit that will maintain consistency and organization. Suggestions on how to best utilize and store the units in this book follow.

Simulation Format

Each simulation begins with a lesson plan designed to assist the teacher with the preparations and procedures necessary and closes with valuable background information which connects the simulation to the historical events being studied. The lesson plan for each simulation follows this format:

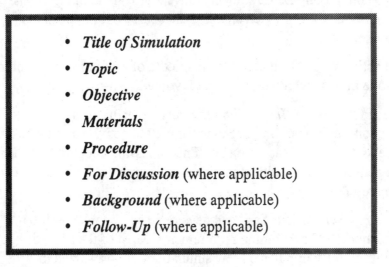

- *Title of Simulation*
- *Topic*
- *Objective*
- *Materials*
- *Procedure*
- *For Discussion* (where applicable)
- *Background* (where applicable)
- *Follow-Up* (where applicable)

Storing Simulations

As you use each activity, you will want to save the components of the simulation by using a readily available and well organized system which will serve the future as well as the present. Labeled file folders or large manila envelopes can be easily sorted and organized by simulation units and kept in a file box. Pages that will be duplicated or made into overhead transparencies can easily be stored in the file folders or envelopes. Game cards, labels, etc., should be placed in envelopes or resealable plastic bags before storing them in their respective folders. If possible, use index paper or heavy stock for reproduced items, such as game pieces, that will be used over and over again. Lamination will help preserve these items.

Outside materials such as candy or plastic spoons should be readily available and noted on the outside of the activity's folder to serve as a reminder that these items need to be accessible for the simulation.

Once the simulations have been organized into a file box, you will be prepared for each unit on a moment's notice.

Let the simulations begin!

Cooperative Learning Teams

Cooperative learning is an important instructional strategy because it can be used as an integral part of many educational processes. It is made-to-order for thinking activities. It acts as a powerful motivational tool.

Many of the activities in this unit involve the cooperative learning process in order to find solutions or come to conclusions regarding the simulations. With this in mind, consider the following four basic components of cooperative learning as you initiate team activities.

1. **In cooperative learning, all group members need to work together to accomplish the task.** No one is finished until the whole group is finished and/or has come to consensus. The task or activity needs to be designed so that members are not simply completing their own part but are working to complete one product together.

2. **Cooperative learning groups should be heterogeneous.** It is helpful to start by organizing groups so that there is a balance of abilities within and between groups. Some of the simulations in this book, however, require a specific type of grouping for cooperative teams in order to achieve the simulation objective. Under such circumstances, a balanced, heterogeneous, cooperative learning team arrangement would not be appropriate for the success of the simulation.

3. **Cooperative learning activities need to be designed so that each student contributes** to the group, and individual group members can be assessed on their performance. This can be accomplished by assigning each member a role that is essential to the completion of the task or activity. When input must be gathered from all members of the group, no one can go along for a free ride.

4. **Cooperative learning teams need to know the social as well as the academic objectives** of a lesson. Students need to know what they are expected to learn and how they are supposed to be working together to accomplish the learning. Students need to process or think and talk about how they worked on social skills as well as to evaluate how well their group worked on accomplishing the academic objective. Social skills are not something that students automatically know; these skills need to be taught.

Artifact Inquiry

Topic

The role of archaeology in helping us to understand history

Objective

Working in groups, students will identify the functions of previously unknown objects by their appearances and/or structures.

Materials

- Bring in one unusual object for each learning team in your class. Basements, attics, yard sales, flea markets, or antique shops are all likely sources for items not readily identifiable for students.

Procedure

1. Divide the class into cooperative learning teams and give each team an object or "artifact" that has been brought to class.

2. Allow each team to examine the objects for about three or four minutes. For example, if you have six learning teams, each team should spend three to four minutes inspecting each of the six items before passing each item on to the next team. After several minutes of examination, teams need to rotate objects in a teacher-directed order so that each team will eventually inspect all items available.

3. Brainstorming is an excellent way for team members to share their ideas on the function of the "artifacts." Reproduce copies of the Brainstorming Web on page 96 and distribute one to each team. Ask team members to complete the webs by writing suggestions of possible functions for each of the items. While giving an exact identity of the objects will be next to impossible, members of each team can use the final minutes of inspection of each "artifact" to delineate some function of that item. Like an archaeologist separated by time from the owner of a relic, the students need to search for clues of how the object was used.

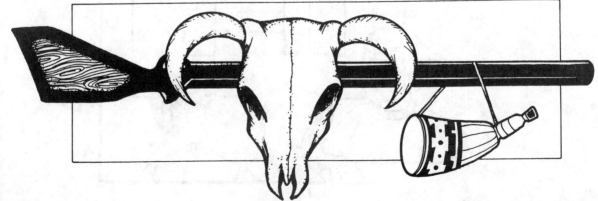

6

Artifact Inquiry *(cont.)*

Procedure *(cont.)*

4. Once all teams have examined all objects, teams can be paired to share their information and ideas. The teacher will then reveal each item's actual name and use(s) to the class. Just as archaeologists put their heads together, groups collectively sharing could very well uncover pertinent ideas not noticed by each individual team before. If students give the approximate function(s) of an object, that alone should count as a success.

Note to the Teacher: In a five minute perusal of a basement workshop, a teacher might have discovered an antique glass furniture coaster, a rubber cap for a kitchen chair leg, a brass-plated ornamental eagle for a lamp post, the cleaning implement for a ramrod to a muzzle-loading rifle, and a metal window jamb pulley for a very old double-hung window. It is highly unlikely that more than one or two (if any) of these objects would ever be correctly placed by the students. However, if they said the eagle was ''screwed on to something for a decoration,'' that would be correct due to its threaded bottom. The idea that something was protected by the rubber cap (a kitchen chair leg) would also be acceptable. Students need not be exact, only close in appropriate function.

Background

When archaeologists dig up artifacts, many times they are unearthing certain objects for the first time and must guess the function based on appearance. Further digs in similar locales may shed more light on these objects and give greater credence to a researcher's proposed identification. ''Artifact Inquiry,'' while not having the benefit of further explorations, is in a way similar to the process involved in archaeology. It is an excellent activity for beginning the year in history since archaeology is a fundamental source of our information on many past events and cultures.

Follow-Up

For those with a real desire to simulate an archaeological dig, bury several related objects in each of several sturdy boxes (again, one box per team). Have students set up a coordinate grid on their box ''sites'' using string or yarn and tacks to hold the string into the side of the box. They should then use spoons and old sieves to carefully remove dirt, and to detail the location of each find. Old pottery broken into several dull-edged pieces may serve very well as the potential relic. Students could attempt to put the pottery back together again.

"Odd Man Out" Trade Review

Topic

Trade patterns within fifteenth century Europe that directly impacted the subsequent "Age of Discovery"

Objective

Students will use this activity to review text-based material on the events leading up to the "Age of Discovery." They will explain why water routes to the Far East were secured by nations such as Portugal and Spain.

Materials

- page 11, reproduced onto index cards or heavy stock (one card per student so that one-third of the class receives cards marked "Asia," one-third receives an "Italy" card, and the remaining third is given cards labeled "Europe")

- pages 12-13, reproduced onto index paper or heavy stock (laminated, if desired) and cut out

- valued reinforcer for your students (This could vary from minutes of extra recess, to M & M's®, to whatever the teacher deems suitable and the students value. See page 93 for additional suggestions.)

- a series of review questions designed to cover the corresponding material from the text

Procedure

1. Randomly distribute the cards labeled "Asia," "Italy," and "Europe" (page 11). In so doing you divide the class into three teams.

"Odd Man Out" Trade Review *(cont.)*

Procedure (cont.)

2. Give students receiving the "Asia" cards ten blue tokens each. Pass out ten red tokens to each recipient of an "Italy" card. (Those students with "Europe" cards receive no tokens at all since historically the European continent was at the mercy of the Italian-Arab connection in respect to Asian trade until the time of the Portugese and Spanish naval explorations.)

3. The tokens represent the valued reinforcer (trade goods) to the students. Each token can be assigned a value the teacher deems appropriate — e.g., one token equals ten M & M's® or two minutes extra recess.

4. Before the game begins, place all disaster cards (page 12) face down on a playing surface. These cards are to be given to "Italy" or "Asia" teams for missed questions. When a question is incorrectly answered, a disaster card is turned over, and the appropriate number of tokens (never more than two) are given to the teacher.

   This central supply of tokens is doled out to teams that may have lost all their tokens but which answer a subsequent question correctly.

5. Starting with the "Asia" team, offer review questions alternately between the "Asia" and "Italy" team members.

6. For a correct response, a token is received from the opposing team. Should the "Europe" team feel left out, and well they should, encourage them by indicating that there are opportunities for their team, also, if they are patient.

7. Anytime the "Italy" team misses a review question, give the "Europe" team the opportunity to answer the missed question. If the "Europe" team correctly identifies that answer, it wins one of the "Italy" team's tokens.

"Odd Man Out" Trade Review *(cont.)*

Procedure (cont.)

8. The game can end as soon as one team loses all its tokens, or it can go for a set time or question limit to determine a winner. However, because the tokens provide a reinforcement to students, they may be motivated to want to keep the game going.

For Discussion

After the game is completed, discuss with the students (especially the "Europe" team members) their frustrations about being left out in the beginning of the game. It is conceivable that with a dominant "Italy" team, the "Europe" team members may have had little opportunity to win tokens. Be sure to drive the point home that those same frustrations were shared by fifteenth century Europeans, as they found it extremely expensive and difficult in trading for the goods they desired from the Near East. Time permitting, cooperative learning teams could brainstorm possible courses of action for countries facing such difficulty.

Background

In the interim between Marco Polo's dramatic return to Italy and Vasco da Gama's voyage around Africa to India, most of Europe was held hostage to a trade monopoly. This enterprise operated out of Middle Eastern cities such as Damascus by way of Genoa and Venice. Merchants from these Italian city-states were able to control the valuable trade with the Asian markets headquartered in the Middle East. The vise-like dominance of the Italian powers eventually led seafaring nations such as Portugal and Spain to methodically search for water routes to the spices, silks, and other riches of the Far East. "Odd Man Out" is designed to review this portion of history with an affective guise where students will feel the sense of frustration and futility in being left out in a "race for riches."

It is important for students to realize that this sense of frustration was the key factor in initiating the "Age of Discovery" and the subsequent settlement of America.

"Odd Man Out" Trade Review
Team Cards

Reproduce as directed on page 8. Color and laminate, if desired.

"Odd Man Out" Trade Review
Disaster Cards

Have the following disaster cards prepared in advance. They stipulate various difficulties that could beset a European trading expedition taking the standard route toward Asian riches — i.e., by way of the Mediterranean Sea and the deserts of the Middle East.

See pages 8 and 9 for directions.

Violent storm ravages your ship. **Lose 2 tokens.**	Water is running desperately low. **Lose 2 tokens.**
Avalanche in mountain pass. Caravan scattered. **Lose 2 tokens.**	Dust storm! **Lose 1 token.**
Pirates attack your ship. **Lose 1 token.**	Bandits harass your caravan **Lose 1 token.**
Your journey has dragged on for over two years. **Lose 2 tokens.**	Caravan travels slowly in sub-zero weather. **Lose 1 token.**

"Odd Man Out" Trade Review Game Markers

Color ten of the markers red and ten markers blue. Laminate for durability, if desired. Cut out markers.

See pages 9 and 10 for directions on use.

Brown Gold

Topic

Spanish colonization of the New World

Objective

Students will identify a major reason for the Spanish colonization of the New World.

Materials

- two bars of chocolate

Procedure

1. Before class begins, hide a bar of chocolate somewhere within your room.

2. Divide the class into cooperative learning teams of two, three, or four students per team. For purposes of this activity varied group sizes may be preferable. Each team should either choose or be assigned a name of a European nation involved in American exploration and/or colonization — i.e., Spain, Portugal, England, France, Sweden, Holland, and Russia.

3. Begin the class by savoring the second luscious bar of chocolate in front of the students. Do not hesitate to detail its delectable qualities in order to produce avid student involvement that will be necessary in the more critical question and answer segment later.

4. Announce to the class that another chocolate bar is hidden somewhere in the classroom. Within their teams, have students discuss their strategies for obtaining the lost bar of ''brown gold.'' Allow only a few minutes for them to ''size up'' the room from their seats.

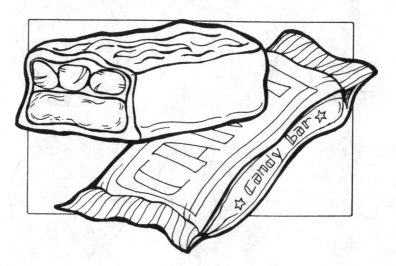

Brown Gold *(cont.)*

Procedure *(cont.)*

5. Be sure to have outlined any necessary ground rules before you begin the actual hunt. Without proper guidance, inappropriate student behavior can negate the very positive goal of this lesson.

6. At the designated signal, allow the students to move about the classroom in search of the missing chocolate bar.

For Discussion

After the "brown gold" has been claimed and divided among the lucky recipients, entertain a discussion wherein the students openly express the feelings they experienced during the quest. (Students may like sitting in a "Sharing" or a "Magic" circle arrangement for purposes of sharing in this discussion.) Introduce the following questions for class discussion:

- What aspect of the teacher's introduction made you want to participate in the search?

- Would you have looked as hard as you did if you knew there was one bar of chocolate out there for everyone?

- Did the limited number of bars make the prize more valuable?

- How did you feel when someone else found the bar?

- Why might this chocolate bar be called "brown gold"?

- If several nations were seeking the same small amount of real gold, how might they try to claim it?

Use the questions above for relating the here-and-now aspects of the lesson back to the driving force behind the Age of Discovery and, specifically, the colonization of the New World. The point of the group numbers may be introduced here. Most notably, if the largest group found the bar of candy, the point needs to be made (despite students' ideas about fairness) that more powerful and better equipped navies had a great advantage in gaining new territory for a nation.

Brown Gold *(cont.)*

For Discussion *(cont.)*

If "Brown Gold" is being used as an anticipatory set, have the students note the following questions and look for their answers as the unit continues:

- What riches were the Spanish interested in?
- Why were the conquistadors so driven to find wealth?
- Did they allow anything (or anyone) to stand in their way?
- Did their actions cause undue suffering to themselves or others? What were the most important effects of the conquistadors actions?

If this activity is being employed for closure/review, the aforementioned questions should go a long way toward meeting that objective.

Background

"Brown Gold" can provide a lively anticipatory set designed to have students experience the excited state of mind that precipitated many of the events during the colonization of the New World and Age of Discovery. When the Spanish conquistadors came to the Americas, they were motivated by the "three G's"— God, glory, and gold. Judging by the millions in gold and silver bullion shipped to Spain, the millions more that ended upon the ocean floor, and the numerous acts of treachery that befell early explorers like Balboa and Pizarro (not to mention the native population), it can be safely assumed that greed was another ever-present "G" that made its mark on this portion of history.

While there were other reasons that need to be investigated to understand the colonization of the Americas by the Spanish and others, the human desire to gain material advantage was a primary consideration. It is a condition that can easily enough be recreated within the classroom in order to make the history of this period relevant to students.

Treasure Map

Topic

Map reading

Objective

Employing a map's key, symbols, and scale, students will read a map of their classroom correctly in order to find a hidden "treasure."

Materials

- an overhead transparency of the blank map on page 20

- one copy per learning team of a completed, detailed classroom map prepared by the teacher, using the blank rectangle on page 20 as a guide

- a valued reinforcer (This can be whatever the teacher deems appropriate as long as students would be excited about it. It should also be small enough to be easily hidden within the classroom. It should also be divisible, since the activity calls for students to work in teams. Fruit, candy, pencils, a notice of extra recess time, etc., are just some of the possibilities. See page 93 for additional suggestions.)

- a text-based lesson on basic map reading skills

- overhead projector

Procedure

1. The teacher needs to hide the chosen reinforcer within the classroom.

2. Assuming you have a traditionally-shaped classroom, use the copy of the map on page 20 (blank rectangle) and place an "X" to mark the hidden item's location. (NOTE: By placing the object near the perimeter of the room, its location will be more obscure. Due to the nature of the activity, that is a favorable characteristic. If your room is not rectangular, it will be necessary to make your own outline.)

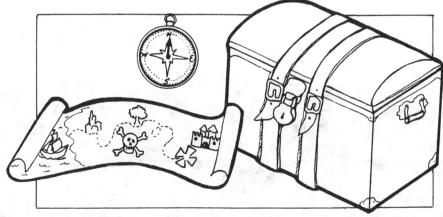

Treasure Map *(cont.)*

Procedure (cont.)

3. On one separate copy of the blank map on page 20, prepare a detailed map of the classroom, including pertinent classroom features (similar to the "Sample Classroom Treasure Map" found on page 19). Reproduce one copy of the detailed map for each team, but do not distribute the map until a team has "earned" it. (See Procedure 7.)

4. Organize students into learning groups or teams for the purposes of this activity.

5. Display on the overhead projector the transparency of the blank map on page 20 (with the solitary "X"). Inform them of the significance of the "X." If the students do not immediately catch on to the map's ambiguity, pose the obvious question — "What is wrong with this map?"

6. Students should be encouraged to also note what features a good map of the classroom would include, such as desks, tables, chalkboard, and aquarium. Note what basic map components are missing as well — e.g., title, key, symbols, scale. Allow students to spend a few minutes discussing these points within their teams before a general class discussion.

7. Before beginning the text's lesson on maps, inform the class that you have a detailed class map to help them find the "treasure." You will award it to any group that correctly responds to review questions about the lesson at its conclusion.

8. All teams that become eligible to search for the "treasure" should be given one copy of the detailed class map you prepared. Allow students within a group one minute to collaborate with their team members before embarking on the search. (Be sure to review behavioral guidelines to keep the search properly disciplined. If more than one team is eligible to search, designate an order whereby only one team searches at a time.)

9. The first team to find the treasure (within the appropriate guidelines) wins it.

Follow-Up

"Treasure Map" is a simple motivator that is designed to reinforce basic map reading skills. It can be easily attached to other areas of the social studies curriculum.

By correlating it with another lesson and its subsequent review questions, "Treasure Map" serves as an anticipatory set for that lesson as well as a general review of map skills.

18

Sample Classroom Treasure Map

See pages 17 and 18 for directions.

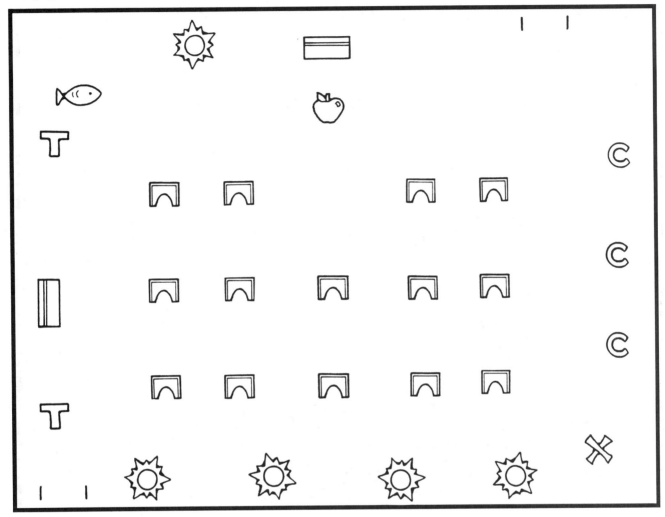

Scale: 1" (2.54 cm) = 5' (1.5 m)

Map Key

🐟	aquarium	T	table
| |	entrance	⊓	student desk
🍎	teacher's desk	C	centers
▭	chalkboard	✕	treasure
☀	window(s)		

Blank Classroom Map

See pages 17 and 18 for directions.

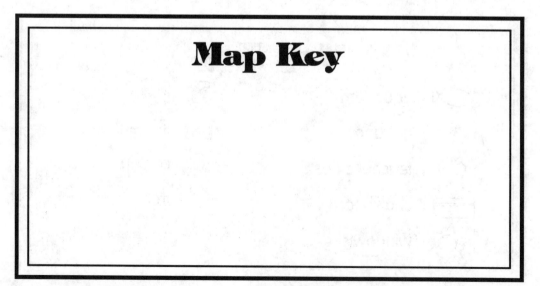

Scale:

Map Key

Coronado's Telephone

Topic

Francisco Coronado's explorations of the American Southwest

Objective

Students will recognize the inherent inaccuracies of second-hand information. They will identify the reason for Francisco Coronado's expedition.

Materials

- page 23, reproduced (one copy per student)

Procedure

1. You will be utilizing the child's game of "telephone" where messages need to be repeated as accurately as possible. Begin by creating a one-sentence message. The subject should be of some interest to the class. (Food topics usually appeal to a great cross-section of any student body.)

2. Explain to the class that while you will be introducing a lesson about the famous Spanish conquistador, Francisco Coronado, they will be quietly circulating an oral message throughout the room. It will be passed from the teacher to a student at one corner of the classroom.

3. From there it will be unobtrusively passed from one student to the next so that no one else can hear it. Meanwhile the students not immediately involved with the message will be attending to the lesson as it is proceeding.

4. When the last student has received the message, have it presented to the teacher. Share the message, as the last student understands it, with the rest of the class.

5. Students will enjoy this activity so much that they will probably want to repeat it. Some repetition will not only be fun but also add further credence to the results of the previous "telephone" message activity. Distribute a copy of page 23 to each student. Ask each student to write a sentence (about seven words) on the page and fold it in half. Divide the class into groups of about eight students. Have each group member in turn start his/her message around the group. Share final messages.

Coronado's Telephone *(cont.)*

For Discussion

Discuss how the content of the final message compares to the original one. What changes were made? Why do you think this happened?

Compare the results of the "telephone" message to the circumstances surrounding the "Cities of Cibola" Coronado was chasing. Ask the class to respond to the following questions:

- Where did Coronado's information come from?

- How many people may have passed this legend along through the years?

- What caused explorers to want to believe these stories?

Background

The results of this activity can be hilarious. While your message should be relatively simple, even a brief statement such as, "The pepperoni pizza served in the cafeteria included mushrooms and onions," may sound like one of the following sentences by the time it is circulated through the class:

"The pepperoni was served with mush."

"The cafeteria's pizza grew onions."

However, that is precisely what Coronado (and many new world explorers from various European nations) did not understand. Lured by legends or misconstrued information passed along to them, and with their eternal lust for riches, leaders like Coronado subjected their subordinates and themselves to many years of deprivation and disaster in search of nonexistent cities of gold. "Coronado's Telephone," while a bit trite, reinforces a sound premise of human communication — information is best derived from its source; the farther removed from that source the less accurate it will probably be. The simulation does this without surrendering much class time beyond the brief implementation and follow-up discussion (which leads the class toward the intended topic of the conquistador's exploration anyway).

22

Telephone "Mess"age

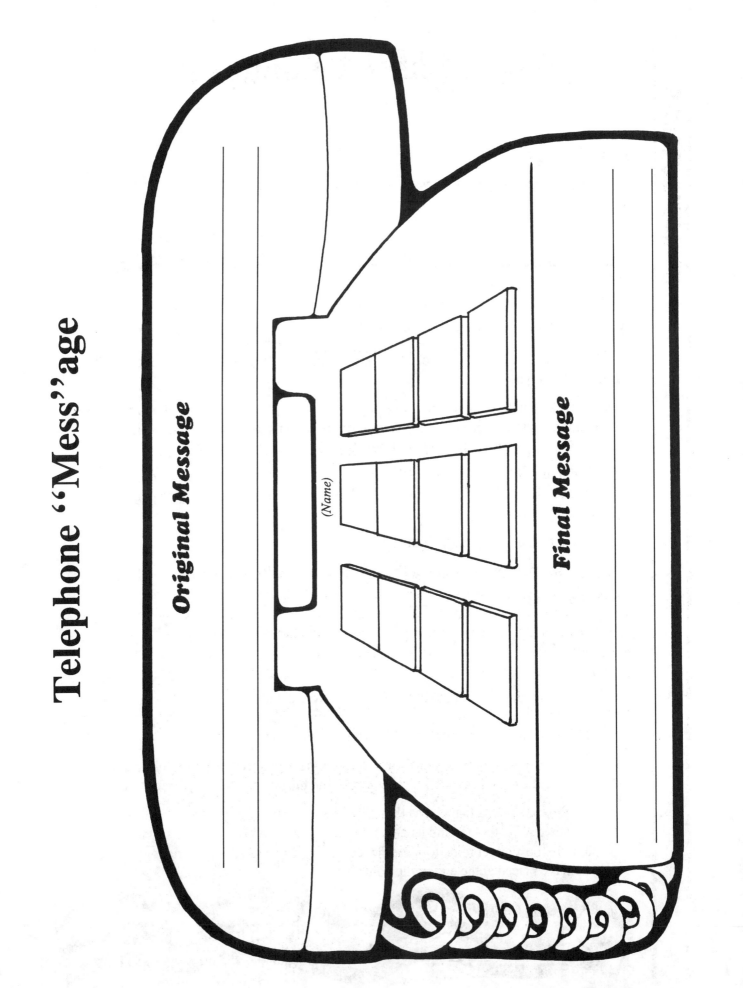

Original Message

(Name)

Final Message

Blind Passage

Topic

The search for the Northwest Passage

Objective

Students will explain why the search for the maritime Northwest Passage was highly prized but never fulfilled during the "Age of Discovery."

Materials

- a large open space such as a school gym (If not available, move student desks to the perimeter of your room.)

- a variety of small, lightweight gym equipment — e.g., floor cones, mobile rubber bases, bowling pins (You will need six to seven of these items for classroom use, eight to ten items if you use one-half of a gym floor.)

- an enticing reward such as baseball cards, a no-homework-night certificate, or any popular classroom reinforcement to be hidden on an obstacle course (See page 93 for additional reward ideas.)

- three bandannas or strips of cloth for blindfolds

- a small slip of paper on which each student will write his/her name

- egg timer or stop watch

Procedure

1. In either the gym, classroom, or school playground, set up an obstacle course utilizing the gym equipment. Since students will be excited while trying to negotiate the course, use equipment they can either step on or easily knock over so no one trips. (See sample course illustration on page 26.) Place the chosen reward on the course.

2. Randomly divide the class into three teams. One team will be named "England," a second team will be named "France," and the third team will be named "Holland."

3. Explain to the class that just as these European nations thought they could find a shortened route to Asia and its coveted trade goods, they (the students) will attempt to find the most direct route to some riches for themselves. (Point to the reward which you have placed at the end of the course.)

24

Blind Passage *(cont.)*

Procedure *(cont.)*

4. Explain that you will require three captains from each team to try to navigate their way, blindfolded, to the riches. To do so, have each willing person put his or her name on a slip of paper and draw three names per team ''out of a hat.''

5. There will be three rounds. In each round, one captain from each nation (team) will start from a different position behind the starting line.

6. The blindfolded captain has one minute to reach his/her reward. As soon as he/she touches an obstacle or goes beyond the course's boundaries, that captain's search is ended.

   (Note: Touching another captain in the race does not disqualify either contestant.)

7. If the first round ends with no one acquiring the reward, begin round two with the next set of captains from each team.

8. However, before the second round begins and after the contestants are blindfolded, rearrange the obstacles. For the subsequent third round, follow the procedures set forth in steps 6 and 7.

9. In order to keep teammates from yelling out assistance, deliver a ten second penalty for any verbal encouragement or directions. This reduces the search time from sixty seconds to fifty seconds and so on for further outbursts.

Background

It is highly unlikely that students will be successful in this endeavor, especially with the strict time limits. Then again, hindsight allows us to recognize the futility of John Cabot's task of locating the Northwest Passage to Asia in 1497. Subsequently, a string of explorers (e.g., Giovanni Verrazano, Jacques Cartier, Henry Hudson, Martin Frobisher) over almost four centuries tried in vain to find this water route. Location of the exact course and the fact that it was frozen most of the year were unknown and inhibiting factors to the early adventurers, many of whose lives were tragically lost in the quest.

Follow-Up

Obviously, the students will meet with a great deal of frustration in this activity. After a teacher-directed discussion outlining the European motives for and realities of such a passage, the teacher may opt to divide the reward among class members anyway. You could create variations of this activity by blindfolding all three captains of one team, having them place their hands on the forward person's waist (like a train) and asking them to try to navigate in such a way. This would place only one team at a time on the course. However, if you choose to do ''Blind Passage,'' always rearrange the course somewhat differently before the next team begins so that no team can have the advantage of memorizing it.

Sample Blind Passage Obstacle Course

Use the sample obstacle course below to help you plan the "Blind Passage" simulation on pages 24-25.

Reward

Key

bowling pin   rubber base   plastic cone

A Question of Tolerance

Topic

The intolerance of Puritans to divergent beliefs and the subsequent settlement of Rhode Island

Objective

Students will identify why Roger Williams and Anne Hutchinson were banished from Massachusetts Bay Colony. Furthermore, they will recognize the effect of this banishment as the start of the new colony of Rhode Island. Students will also realize that it is as important to listen to a different opinion as it is to question it.

Materials

- page 30, reproduced (one copy for each student)

Procedure

1. Present the problem situation on page 30 to the class.

2. Divide the class into cooperative learning groups. Choose one of the following techniques to analyze and discuss the situation.

   - Have teams of four students pair up and share, in partners of two, their possible solutions to the situation on page 30. Afterward, teams should reconvene to discuss their ideas and opinions.

   - Teams may share solutions with one other team, or they may choose a spokesperson to share the ideas of the team with the entire class.

A Question of Tolerance *(cont.)*

For Discussion

It would be very difficult to predetermine what prevailing opinion will arise (if any) in the situation described on page 30. Those very familiar with the Ryan White case may be very sympathetic to the plight of the fictitious youth. Others may not be. Consensus is not the optimum goal for this exercise. What is critical is that the students begin to realize the dynamics of divergent views on an issue. If you use role playing, note if there were attempts at meaningful discussion or whether there were just unfounded accusations hurled at each side. Consider the following questions:

- Did each side really attempt to understand the other side's viewpoint?
- What emotions played an important part for each side?
- Was there a serious attempt to reach a workable compromise?

Total agreement is usually a fantasy. Listening to an opposing viewpoint and constructively trying to deal with it, while not often easy, is a worthy goal.

If the activity is used as an anticipatory set for the study of the settling of New England colonies, ask the students to note the differences between the Puritans of Massachusetts and those people opposed to their strict rule (Roger Williams and Anne Hutchinson). Discuss the factors that may have dictated the Puritan point of view?

''A Question of Tolerance'' could also be used to conclude the same topic with students drawing comparisons between the modern dilemma and the colonial issues they just studied.

28

A Question of Tolerance *(cont.)*

Background

The Puritans came to America seeking to free themselves from the religious oppression they felt plagued them in England. However, once established as masters of the Massachusetts Bay Colony, they were quite reluctant to offer religious freedom to anyone opposing their theological or political perspective.

Individuals such as Roger Williams and Anne Hutchinson dared to speak out against church doctrine and authority in matters like the ethical dealings with Native Americans in procurement of land as well as other topics. History records that both fled their persecutors and set up settlements in what would become the tolerant colony of Rhode Island.

In order to drive home to our students the importance of these forward-thinking colonists, we must look at a contemporary issue that they might actually have to wrestle with at some point in time. The views of Roger Williams and Anne Hutchinson were regarded as radical and not welcomed by most Puritan leaders. Students need to react to a somewhat controversial issue to begin to appreciate the conflict of opinions these early activists faced. Other ''hot'' topics such as women's rights, civil rights, military expenditures, or the environment could be substituted for the one used in this anticipatory set.

Follow-Up

After having introduced Williams and Hutchinson, perhaps a similar discussion or role play situation could be constructed involving their dispute with the Puritan authorities. Hopefully, concerns on both sides would be brought out by the participating students. While Puritans have been held up as a model of intolerance, their previous persecutions and frontier struggles need to be examined next to their ambitions for land and control. In order to nurture a more tolerant and discerning society, students must be given the opportunity to question and listen to the opinions of others.

The Public Concern

The Situation

Rick Smith is a ten-year-old AIDS patient who has recently moved into the neighborhood. His parents would like him to have as normal a childhood as possible and want him to attend the local public school, Fieldstone Elementary. The principal, John Moyers, is in favor of having Rick attend his school. However, Mrs. Janet Page, Mrs. Harriet Drake, and Mr. James Face, all prominent P.T.A. members and community leaders, are opposed to the idea. They say the boy is a threat to the safety and well-being of every other child in the school. They are sympathetic to his plight, but they say their concerns are with the welfare of the rest of the students.

Principal Moyers believes he can work Rick into school with few problems, and he thinks the parental leaders are over-reacting. The P.T.A. and community leaders say Mr. Moyers doesn't fully understand and appreciate the dangers and risks involved.

Question to Consider

What do you think should be done in this situation?

Reprieve Granted

Topic

The settling of the colony of Georgia

Objective

Students will identify the background of the settlers of the colony of Georgia and recognize the reason for its settlement.

Materials

- None

Procedure

1. Arrange your daily schedule so that social studies will be toward the end of the day. (If you are teaching in a departmentalized situation, see Procedure 2.)

2. At some point earlier in the day assign the students a truly enormous work load in one or several subjects. Justify it by telling them the class has to accelerate its work load in order to successfully "cover" required annual topics in the related subject(s). Overplay the necessity of this intensely. The students should be in utter agony over the assignment(s). For those social studies teachers in a departmentalized setting, try to arrange such an assignment with one or more colleagues who would have had your students earlier in the day.

3. If your classroom is self-contained, inform the class at the start of social studies that you have had a certain change of heart concerning that day's work load. Should they respond well to the lesson about the southern colonies, you might reduce their other assignment(s). (Departmentalized teachers see Procedure 6.)

4. Proceed with your lesson in social studies. There should be a keen interest in the lesson, given the potential stake the class has in it.

5. After a review of the lesson, announce to the class that due to their progress on this lesson, you will reduce their homework in the other area(s) to whatever the normal assignment would be.

Reprieve Granted *(cont.)*

Procedure *(cont.)*

6. Those of you in a departmentalized situation should probably select only one later class (one that has been together for the entire academic day). Innocently ask how their day has gone in order to flush out their contempt for the inordinate work load. Tell the class that perhaps you can intercede for them provided they work well for you as you begin study of the southern colonies. Proceed with your lesson in social studies. After a review of the lesson, make the announcement that the homework assignment(s) will return to "normal."

For Discussion

Discuss with the class how they feel about their end-of-day reprieve, using the following questions:

- How did it feel to have that kind of pressure placed on you to potentially complete that much work?

- What were your feelings towards the assignment? the instructor? Did any of you feel so overwhelmed by it that you felt like just giving up?

- Did you feel more motivated to do your social studies?

- How did it feel to win the reduced assignment?

Introduce the topic of Georgia's settlement by transferring the students' recently won pardon to that similar reprieve gained by English debtors who were able to start anew across the Atlantic in James Oglethorpe's Georgia. (See Background.) If possible, once the material has been covered, have students compare their dilemma with that of the newly pardoned debtors back in 1732.

Reprieve Granted *(cont.)*

For Discussion *(cont.)*

Note to the teacher: Be sure you leave enough time before the end of the day (or class period) to cover all important procedures and discussion points. Do not let the day (or class period) end with the students still believing that they must do the extra work load assignment. Emphasize that this activity was a simulation.

Background

The settlement of Georgia in 1732 was an altruist's dream come true. Yet, there were practical politics behind it. Philanthropists led by James Oglethorpe wanted to secure a colony for worthy individuals mired in England's debtors' prisons. Instead of wasting human ambition behind bars, Oglethorpe's group believed a new start in America would be the ideal solution for these people many of whose only "crime" was not having enough money to live on.

As a statesman, Oglethorpe also knew that Parliament would take to the plan in order to protect the prosperous rice and indigo plantations of the Carolinas from the Spanish threat in Florida. Even though slavery and liquor were outlawed, and only wine and silk were to be produced, within two decades Georgia's economy was assimilated into the slavery-dependent cash crop-producing economy of its northern neighbors.

The King's M & M's®

Topic

Colonial America's reaction to the Stamp Act

Objective

Students will explain why Americans were upset with British tax laws, such as the Stamp Act, after the French and Indian War. They will also identify two tactics colonials used to demonstrate their displeasure with these taxes.

Materials

- one 8 ounce (224grams) bag of M & M's®

- pages 37-39, reproduced on index paper or heavy stock

- one small paper cup for each student

- two plastic spoons (or surgical latex gloves)

Procedures

1. Prepare the Role Cards as directed on pages 37-38.

2. Cut out the Object Cards on page 39. Label the six cards with names of items commonly worn or possessed by students within class — e.g., jeans, running shoes, glasses, pens, jewelry. You do not need to use all six cards; three to six cards seem to work well for this simulation. In the corner box of each of the object cards, write a number ranging from one to three. As will be explained later, these numbers will represent a taxable value.

3. At the start of class give each student a paper cup containing ten M & M's®. Instruct students not to touch them.

The King's M & M's® *(cont.)*

Procedure (cont.)

4. Randomly pass out the role cards to students. Explain that those possessing the "King," "Parliament," and "Tax Collector" cards should proceed to the front of the room. The king should take a designated "seat of honor," and the members of Parliament should also have a specific area from which they will enact their roles.

5. Members of Parliament (those students possessing "Parliament" Role Cards) will draw from your previously compiled and prepared group of Object Cards. Parliament members announce to the "Colonists" what item is to be taxed (e.g., blue jeans), and anyone possessing that item will have to pay out the number of M & M's equal to the number written on the object card. So if the card marked "blue jeans — 3" is pulled, each colonist attired in blue jeans would relinquish three M & M's®.

6. Those students possessing "Tax Collector" role cards do all of the collecting using plastic spoons or gloves and all "taxes" are returned to Parliament. (Each tax collector has charge over half the room.) Taxes should be levied for at least three items but not more than six. If you have a good idea of what is popular in student dress, four items seems to be an optimum number for successfully relieving several students of all their candy and leaving many more with just two or three of their original total.

7. After all taxes have been levied, the funds are to be dispersed. The tax collectors each reap 10% of the take. Parliament receives 50% (these funds to be used to run the empire) to be split equally among the two students in that role. Finally, King George pockets the remaining 40% for himself. (These percentages have no real historical significance and are only an arbitrary breakdown for purposes to fit this simulation.) It is quite possible that while some students will have had all of their M & M's® confiscated, members of Parliament and the king will have upwards of thirty to forty pieces each to show for their efforts.

The King's M & M's® *(cont.)*

Procedure *(cont.)*

8. Some students may show definite feelings of displeasure just as some on the receiving end of this taxing generosity may gloat just a bit too much. The objective for this lesson should be completed during the withdrawal from the roles.

For Discussion

Understanding how the colonists reacted to the tax collectors and the various tax laws from the Stamp Act and beyond will be more relevant to the class at this crucial moment. Discuss the following questions:

- What was so unfair about how the class was taxed?

- How could it have been handled more fairly?

- Why were tax collectors tarred and feathered?

- Why were British goods boycotted?

- What methods and organizations were devised by the colonists in order to resist and circumvent these laws?

- How significant were these laws to the ultimate break from Great Britain?

Background

While it can be used as an anticipatory set, "The King's M & M's®" is most effective in the discussion about the Stamp Act after the topic has been introduced and formally presented. Sufficient background makes post-simulation review more meaningful. Since the colonists were upset about new taxes on paper and the lack of representation in the establishment of those taxes, this strategic activity attempts to draw students into a similar, albeit contrived, situation where items they value are arbitrarily removed from their possession without their input.

The students' frustration with the "unfairness" of the way they lost their candy can be easily compared to the substantial give and take on one of the central issues leading to revolution — taxation without representation.

Role Cards

Cut out, color, and laminate (if desired), the role cards below. See pages 34-36 for directions on the use of the role cards.

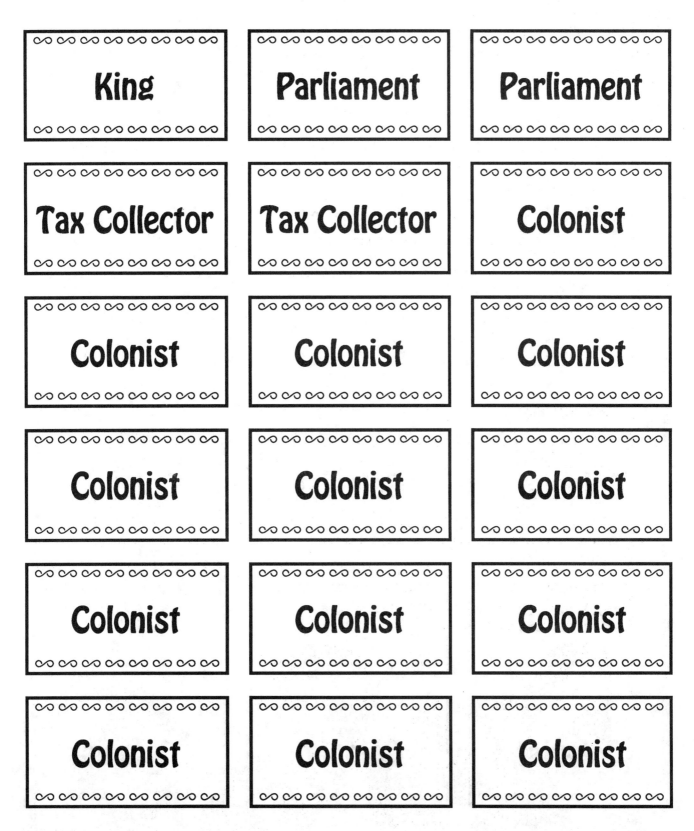

King	Parliament	Parliament
Tax Collector	Tax Collector	Colonist
Colonist	Colonist	Colonist
Colonist	Colonist	Colonist
Colonist	Colonist	Colonist
Colonist	Colonist	Colonist

Role Cards *(cont.)*

Cut out, color, and laminate (if desired), the role cards below. See pages 34-36 for directions on the use of the role cards.

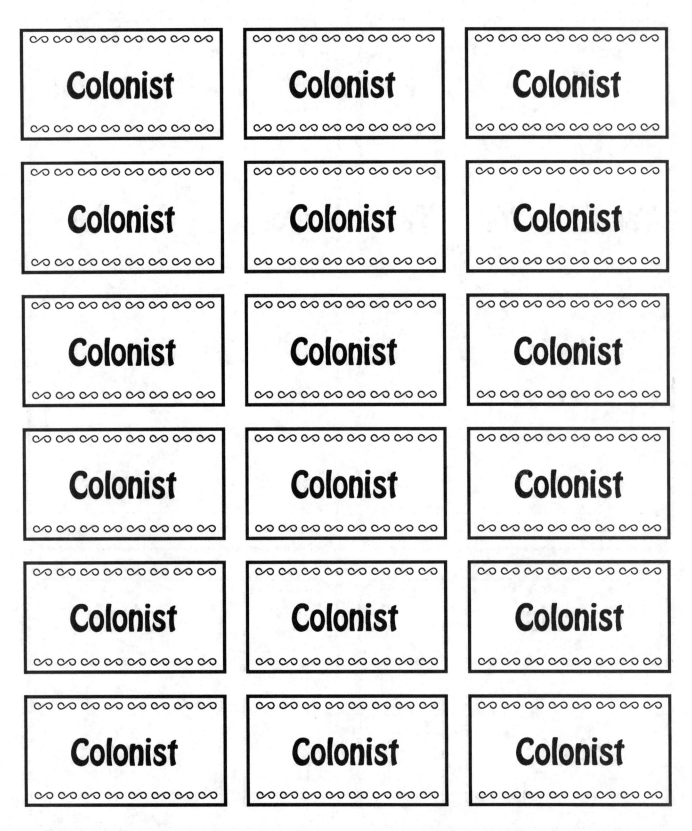

Object Cards

See pages 34 and 35 for directions.

(item)

(item)

(item)

(item)

(item)

(item)

I Spy

Topic

The Revolutionary War

Objective

Students will work in teams to collect information on major personages of the Revolutionary War. Students will identify the major British and American civil and military leaders during the war.

Materials

- Using your social studies text, compile a list of the major people associated with the Revolutionary War (British, French, American) and provide one copy per student.

- For each name on the compiled list, prepare an index card with that name on it.

- page 42, reproduced (one copy per team for each set of questions)

Procedure

1. Have the class arranged in cooperative learning teams.

2. Each student is given a list of about twenty famous individuals from the Revolutionary War. (If at all possible, have the same number of famous people as members in the class. If this can not be arranged, some identities will be used twice within the same class.)

3. Within each team, the list should be divided among the members who are to note the importance of each person on the list in relationship to the War of Independence. Students are to research those historical figures on the list. (For a list of twenty names, each team member in a group of four would be responsible for researching five people.)

4. After an appropriate time for information gathering, groups re-form to share the vital ''intelligence report'' each member has gathered on the historical figures. This cooperative compilation of a ''dossier'' is crucial to the success of the team's mission.

I Spy *(cont.)*

Procedure (cont.)

5. After the teacher feels sufficient time has been given for research and sharing of information within each team, the activity begins. Each student is given an identity card (the index card with the name of one famous person under study on it), and the student assumes the role of this figure during a planned question and answer session. This session may be spread over a period of days or may be concentrated into one or two class periods. You may prefer to extend the activity over several days as it does a remarkable job of keeping students on task and involved throughout the unit.

6. Provide each team with a copy of page 42. Each team is allotted five or six questions a day that they may ask to any student within the class (excluding their own teammates, whose identities are already known to them). The questions must be ones that can be answered with a simple ''Yes'' or ''No.'' The six questions may be centered on one individual or spread out over six people. Each team must decide on five or six questions they would like to ask. Have student teams write their question sets on page 42, along with the responses they received and any comments, notes, or clues the team formulates. Encourage students to take notes and keep track of those individuals already captured. As students sharpen their listening and note-taking skills, information starts to fall into place as to who the historical figure is.

7. When one team successfully guesses another student's identity, that team is awarded a point under whatever reinforcement schedule the instructor is utilizing.

8. If a student gives an incorrect answer about his/her identity, that team receives a warning. Another such mistake from that team warrants a one-point penalty reduction.

9. The competition can be solely to see which team captures the most outstanding historical roles within the class, or it can be tied into other ongoing goals that teams have set for that unit. You may wish to reward the last person to be identified several bonus points for being able to withstand the ''intelligence sweep'' for that long.

Background

Students possess a certain amount of affinity towards the idea of espionage. Perhaps it is the lure of the ''James Bond'' or ''Mission Impossible'' mystique. It could be that to be a spy requires a certain amount of cunning and wit. ''I Spy'' makes use of this attraction in order for students to learn more about the significant people associated with the Revolutionary War or any other major American or international conflict.

I Spy Questions and Clues

Team members: _____

_____

Date: _____

Questions asked of the following class/team member(s): _____

_____

Questions   Yes   No

                                                         (Check ☑ response)

1. _____   ☐   ☐

   _____

2. _____   ☐   ☐

   _____

3. _____   ☐   ☐

   _____

4. _____   ☐   ☐

   _____

5. _____   ☐   ☐

   _____

6. _____   ☐   ☐

   _____

Team Notes (List any clues, comments, or special notes regarding the other team's responses.)

_____

_____

_____

_____

Our guess is that the famous historical figure is _____

Consensus

Topic

The Articles of Confederation

Objective

Students will explain why the Articles of Confederation failed to properly govern the newly formed United States. They will also identify what took its place.

Materials

- None

Procedure

1. "Bait" this anticipatory set by grouping students in advance. Pre-established cooperative learning teams would be excellent but not absolutely necessary.

2. Ask the class, "If you had an extra ten minutes of recess today, what one activity would your group decide to do as a group?"

3. Most groups will be able to specify a particular activity in relatively short order without too much squabbling. Once these teams are in agreement, let each group announce its choice to the class.

4. Then say, "Now, I'd like the entire class to decide upon one activity that everyone will participate in if given ten minutes extra recess."

5. Sit back and observe passively. The dynamics of what you witness will be important for the following discussion. Is any one student trying to organize the class in order to bring it to consensus? Is there a myriad of ideas brought forth as to what to do? Are previous group activity selections being honored or fragmented? Are students striving to compromise by working toward an activity all can enjoy in some way? Do the students seem frustrated by the process? If so, don't let the tumult be overly boisterous or last longer than five minutes. (If genuine progress is being accomplished with a minimum of agitation, allow a reasonable opportunity for the process to succeed.)

6. Have the students return to their seats and discuss the feelings they encountered in trying to reach agreement on an activity using the following questions:

   - What problems were you faced with in trying to reach an agreement?

   - Why do you think that as a small group you could function toward a goal, but once you had to decide as a class, you found it more difficult?

Consensus (cont.)

Procedure (cont.)

7. At this point, introduce the scenario facing the United States upon its inception between 1781 and 1789. Begin the text lesson on the Articles of Confederation.

8. By the end of the lesson, students should be able to note the similarities between their inability to agree to a specific activity and the new states not being in unison among themselves.

For Discussion

Compare your observations in Procedure 5 with the turmoil under the Articles of Confederation. Questions such as the following will enhance the students' understanding:

• Just as you could not agree on a recess activity, what were some things the newly independent states could not agree on?

• As you wanted to maintain your position about what activity to enjoy, what kinds of things did the states do to each other to try to make sure no one would boss them around again as England had done?

Background

Consensus is easy to talk about but difficult to reach. As hard as it may be for adults to attain total agreement, often it is more challenging for children.

In mentioning the travails of the thirteen states which acted as thirteen nations, the comparison needs to be drawn to the interpersonal dynamics that had dominated the classroom just minutes ago.

Lack of consensus spelled doom for this nation's initial governing system, the Articles of Confederation. With states printing their own currency (valid within their borders only), taxing out-of-state goods, and failing to contribute to the national treasury funds necessary for the federal government to operate, the failure to procure unified cooperation almost sank the fledgling democracy before it was righted by the Constitution.

Follow-Up

Granting of the extra recess should be made at your discretion. Be advised that throughout the simulation, the teacher needs only to emphasize the possibility of reward. Remain mum about its fate until after the lesson is over and then announce your decision.

Land Grab

Topic

Northwest Ordinance of 1787

Objective

Students will describe how land was parceled out in the settling of the Northwest Territory.

Materials

- one or more county road maps

- an overhead transparency of the township map (Figure #2) on page 48.

- one copy per student of a township-divided county similar to Figure #1 on page 47 (This replaces the county road maps if your section of the country does not utilize township land division.)

- overhead projector

- an overhead transparency of page 47

- butcher paper

Procedure

1. Organize students into cooperative learning teams.

2. Initiate a unit on the formative years of the United States by asking your pupils in what township they live. With the assistance of a county road map, introduce the various townships of your county. In all probability, that county map is already subdivided into sections within each township (especially if you live in the Midwest). They would be numbered 1 to 36 with the first section being in the northeast corner of the township. Due to the later formation of county boundaries, not all townships in every county will be a perfect square and so will not contain an exact 36 sections. If you do not live in an area where townships were a means of settlement, create your own map using the grid on page 47 to represent a county with sixteen townships. Make a transparency of Figure #1 and project it onto butcher paper using an overhead projector. Copy the county map for a bulletin board display in which teams will acquire townships. (See procedure 3.)

Land Grab *(cont.)*

Procedure *(cont.)*

3. Incorporate a unit-long (or any period of time a certain grouping of teams would be together) reinforcement track by having cooperative teams "earn" as many sections as they can on their actual county map or a fictitious county map the teacher creates.

4. For each reinforcement point, either academic or social, the group acquires one section of a township. Each team can choose to start in a different township and see how many sections they can claim as their own throughout the time period they are together as a team. Using the bulletin board county map display, or a real county map, have teams use various colors to indicate their ownership of sections throughout the county. Provide a color-coded map key.

5. Each teacher must decide if and how "sections" are to be redeemed for more tangible rewards.

Background

The Northwest Ordinance of 1787 was the new American government's first major step at populating its vast western frontier. Drawing upon the Land Ordinance of 1785, it divided land into townships, each a six-mile square equaling thirty-six square miles or sections. Each section was made up of 640 acres. During the settlement of the Northwest Territory (from 1788 on through the 1820's), the states of Ohio, Michigan, Indiana, Illinois, and Wisconsin were carved out of the wilderness in this fashion. Congress had hoped to reap major dividends by setting up a one-section minimum purchase for at least one dollar an acre. Since few settlers had six-hundred forty dollars, the land was eventually sold to speculators for mere pennies on the dollar. Eventually, Congress reformed the Land Ordinance to allow individuals to buy quarter or half-sections. Section #15 in each township was reserved for schools.

Follow-Up

Considering that competition among groups should not be overly exploited, a cooperative class goal can be encouraged. So while in selected individual activities teams may compete against each other, perhaps the entire class could have as a goal the complete ownership of "the county." When the county map is totally purchased with reinforcement points (as signified by the color-coded key), the class could share some special reward.

Whether your teams acquire reinforcement points (sections) by themselves or as a class, it becomes an easy way for them to track their achievement. Furthermore, it reinforces the township structuring of the Northwest Ordinance over the course of your unit.

Figure #1

See pages 45 and 46 for directions on how to use the grid below.

Note to the teacher: After the grid has been enlarged and displayed, number each subdivision using page 48 as a guide. You may wish to indicate the location of several towns on the map.

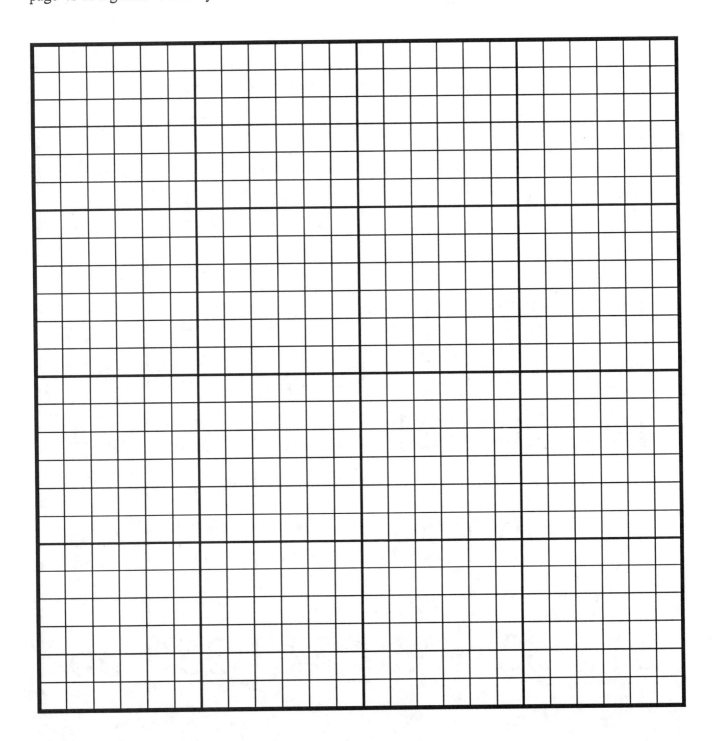

Figure #2

A Sectioned-off Township

See pages 45 and 46 for directions.

6	5	4	3	2	1
7	8	9	10	11	12
18	17	16	15	14	13
19	20	21	22	23	24
30	29	28	27	26	25
31	32	33	34	35	36

Compromise

Topic

The "Great Compromise" of the Constitutional Convention

Objective

Students will recognize what the "Great Compromise" accomplished.

Materials

- paper and pencils

Procedure

1. Divide the class into four or five groups with an unequal number of students in each group. Have one large group of six or seven students, another of four or five, and several smaller ones of two or three.

2. Explain to the class that they will be playing "Circle of Knowledge" where each group is given a specified time limit to list as many items for a teacher-initiated category as possible. For instance, "In the next two minutes, list the last names of as many presidents as your team can." (There should be one recorder for each team writing down its response.) This is an excellent review activity and can be applied to all academic areas. Another sample item for those teachers that employ study guides would be, "In one minute, list all of the things your group learned about (whatever topic) in section one of the study guide."

3. Before actual play begins, set a limit as to the number of lists you will offer, and state that whichever group totals the most correct items after those lists are completed will win. The reward can be a pack of gum, a small box of raisins, or extra recess time. (See additional suggestions on page 93.)

4. It will not take too long for the smaller groups to realize that they are at a distinct disadvantage. It will be common for protests to be raised — "That's not fair; we only had three people in our group. They have six." Vociferous indignation really develops when it appears that a reward is forthcoming.

Compromise *(cont.)*

For Discussion

At this crucial point, ask the class to reach a mutual accord. Initiate discussion with the following question:

- You feel that you have been dealt with unjustly. What does the class think should be done to satisfy as many of its members as possible that they have been treated fairly?

The students will have to debate that for a portion of time. While most will recognize the impropriety of the group sizes, the large group will undoubtedly want to claim the reward. The teacher needs to act as a moderator to guide the pupils into some mutually defined settlement. This process need not drag on for more than five to ten minutes. The importance lies in the idea that in the end, a large majority of the class (including the winning team) feels it has received a fair deal.

Background

Lead the students into the next lesson about the Constitutional Convention. Be sure to point out that in a case not unlike the one the class just underwent, the Founding Fathers' ability to compromise insured the confirmation of our nation's legal backbone.

Compromise is a daily fact of life. American history is punctuated with numerous compromises of monumental stature such as the Missouri Compromise and the Compromise of 1850. In fact, it took the ''Great Compromise'' to help give birth to the Constitution. Similar to the simulation described above, small states did not want to cave in to the demands of more populated states so that population alone would carry the weight in the newly designed government.

After much debate, a bicameral legislature was established with one house based on equal representation (Senate) and the other on population (House of Representatives).

Beyond its historical and political context, as previously noted, compromise is part of everyday life. Those who insist on having their own way may find themselves momentary winners, but long-term losers shut out from the mainstream, unable to mesh socially. In the adult world, studies have shown that as many as 85% of terminated business executives were released for an inability to cooperate rather than for reasons of incompetence.

50

Widget Assembly

Topic

Introduction to the rise of mass production and its effect on the Industrial Revolution

Objective

Students will be able to explain why interchangeable parts helped factories develop and lessened the role of individual craftsmen in American business.

Materials

- several boxes of toothpicks
- one shoe box full of styrofoam packing chips
- page 54, reproduced (one copy per student)

Procedure

1. Divide the class into several groups of four students each with two or three selected students left over who would be willing to work on their own.

2. Share with the class a model of a "widget." (See diagram on page 54.) This model is constructed from toothpicks and styrofoam packing chips. Since the function and purpose of the "widget" as a product is not the issue here, the teacher does not need to dwell on the finished product but rather the process under which it is made. You may wish to simulate its function by saying that the "widget" will be an approximate model of a device used to "... test wind resistance in a certain technological research project." If you are uncomfortable with this approach, create any other simple structure from readily available items and make up your own rationale for its existence.

Widget Assembly *(cont.)*

Procedure (cont.)

3. Students are to be instructed on how the device should be put together. The groups will be working cooperatively and by themselves in order to make the most quality pieces possible in a fifteen-minute period.

   (If you choose, you may prefer to offer a simple incentive for the highest number of quality pieces made. However, be advised to set stringent guidelines as to the time allotted and product specifications if you undertake this approach.) Quality control on this product needs to focus on following the exact model given on the blueprint. There may be a variance allowed by the teacher since he/she will have the final say on the acceptability of each piece.

4. Allow each team/individual five minutes to ready materials and production procedure. No pieces may be constructed yet.

5. Let production begin. After fifteen minutes, get an accurate count of the number of quality pieces created by each group or individual.

For Discussion

Display the totals on an overhead projector or blackboard and discuss the results with the class by asking the following questions:

- Who made the most?

- Was there a difference in quality? (If there is a distinct discrepancy in quality, the teacher needs to address it now in order to clarify the total count to any groups that had defective pieces.)

Widget Assembly *(cont.)*

For Discussion *(cont.)*

- Were the bad pieces produced as a result of poor material or management (i.e., adhering to directions)?

- If you were a customer interested in placing a large order for "widgets," to which group would you give your business and why?

Lead into the next lesson about Whitney's development of interchangeable parts. Be sure to draw on the students' experience with "widgets" to help them see how manufacturing in the United States began to evolve.

Background

This activity's focus is to note the importance of the rise of mass production initiated by Eli Whitney's invention of interchangeable parts.

Upon independence, the United States was an agrarian society with individual craftsmen supplying the needs of the farming populace. Within half a century, factories were taking over the bulk of the manufacturing of goods from textiles to guns. One hundred years later, Henry Ford took a European idea, the automobile, and made it into the invention of the century through similar means of mass production. "Widget Assembly" provides the tactile modality in which to transmit this concept.

Blueprint of a "Widget"

Directions: Make each "widget" using the model below. With the exception of the two middle chips in each row, all toothpicks need to be embedded in the styrofoam chips without protruding through the other side of the chips.

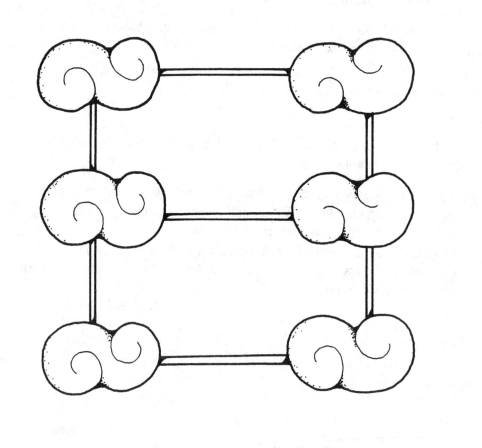

Hands Off!

Topic

The Monroe Doctrine

Objective

Students will explain what the Monroe Doctrine said and why President Monroe wrote it.

Materials

- classroom world map or transparency of world map on page 95
- page 57, reproduced (one copy for each student)

Procedure

1. Have students grouped in cooperative learning groups.

2. Present the problem-solving situation (page 57) to the class.

3. Allow teams five to ten minutes to discuss the situation within their groups.

4. Engage the students in a general class discussion based on what they shared within their teams. Students who believe the neighborhood patrols can work in ''The Defenders'' Dilemma may list several legitimate sources of power that make such a movement effective — e.g., massive citizen involvement and pride, police and community working side by side, criminal perspective that the ''pickings'' would be better elsewhere when confronted by community action. Depending upon the students' environment, they may disagree and feel such a program would have limited success.

For Discussion

Whatever the students' viewpoints, transfer the setting from the present to the past with the aid of the world map. Make the western hemisphere analogous to the entire city in ''Hands Off!'' and the United States of 1823 as one neighborhood within it.

Hands Off! *(cont.)*

For Discussion *(cont.)*

Explain how President James Monroe told the powers of Europe to stay out of the western hemisphere or face American resistance.

Discuss the following question:

- How could President Monroe have made such a charge in 1823 when the United States was still young and with only limited military resources?

Proceed with the next lesson pertaining to the Monroe Doctrine.

Background

While the problem-solving situation is very limited in scope and very contemporary in setting, it still remains very similar to the backdrop of the Monroe Doctrine. By 1823, the United States was being viewed abroad as a stable, if not powerful, nation. Concerned about the fledgling democracies, the opportunity for trade with these novice republics, and the threat of European monarchies (Spain, France) regaining a foothold in these areas, Monroe was prompted to make his famous edict in an address to Congress. As often as this address has been used by various American administrations to intervene in numerous locales from the Dominican Republic to Nicaragua, the initial power behind the 1823 proclamation was not that of the United States. Rather, Great Britain saw innumerable economic advantages in trading with the new nations, and her navy — the scourge of the seas — was the inaugural enforcement of the Monroe Doctrine.

As an anticipatory set to the study of the Monroe Doctrine, ''Hands Off!'' is designed to stimulate students to think about an immense concern involving human rights encompassing a large area. On the surface, the Monroe Doctrine would seem to have been a rather brazen statement in 1823, emanating from a leader of nation less that fifty years old. That he would dictate an entire hemisphere of the globe was off limits for the European powers of the day would, at face value, be ludicrous. However, just as there are potentially mitigating factors that students may very well consider in the problem-solving situation, Great Britain's trade interests were such that no other government of the time wanted to provoke Britannia, ruler of the seas.

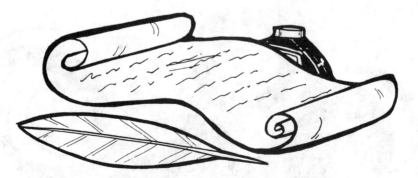

56

"The Defenders" Dilemma

The Situation

"The Defenders" is a community-organized crime prevention patrol for a large inner-city neighborhood. Ten groups of three to five unarmed volunteers patrol their neighborhood streets throughout the night. They have been successful in sharply reducing crime, especially gang-related activities. Just because they are there, violence has dwindled to only a few acts a month.

"The Defenders" neighborhood is about one-tenth the area of the city. Recently, however, the leaders of "The Defenders" have said that criminals, most notably gang leaders, had better just leave town altogether. They mentioned that the entire city would be off limits to gangs and, if need be, "The Defenders" would go city-wide to back up this threat.

Having successfully controlled their own neighborhood (which is only one-tenth of the city), do you think a patrol group such as "The Defenders" can actually follow through on a claim to make the entire city safe? If so, what groups of people are there that will fully support "The Defenders" and help enforce their city-wide cause? Who would benefit from such a plan of safe streets?

Questions to Consider

If you do not think the threat of "The Defenders" will stop gangs and crime, why not?

What things will exist that will keep such a plan from working out throughout the city?

The Heartbreak of Pioneering

Topic

Westward expansion in the United States (Manifest Destiny)

Objective

Students will identify one reason Easterners moved to the frontier of the American West during the middle of the nineteenth century.

Material

- page 60, reproduced (one copy per student)

Procedure

1. Assign students to cooperative learning groups with four students to a team if possible.

2. Present them with the problem-solving dilemma.

3. Divide the class into groups. Allow groups some time to reread and think about the problem. Then, ask each student within his/her group to voice a solution to "The Plight of the Pioneer."

4. Allow the groups five to ten minutes to think about and come up with possible solutions. Afterwards, have a team spokesperson from each group share the group's thoughts with the class.

5. While a definitive solution may prove difficult to reach, the center of the students' attention is upon the life and death struggles that so characterized existence on the American frontier. Individuals with contented, comfortable lives did not usually risk their lifestyle against the odds of survival in the West. Generally speaking, those with little to look forward to in life thought it worth the risk to start anew in what became known as this land's "Manifest Destiny."

58

The Heartbreak of Pioneering *(cont.)*

For Discussion

Before beginning the text lesson about westward expansion, direct the questioning to present-day America by discussing the following:

- Where in this land of ours would you find a large portion of people who have little to look forward to in life?

- What have been some risks available to them (positive or negative) in seeking their way out?

Are there true frontiers left to settle, figuratively or literally? The plight of the underprivileged (e.g., the homeless, dwellers of inner-city ghettos, the rural poor, the unemployed) could easily be mentioned. Furthermore, various attempted avenues out of their impoverishment could be brought up, such as governmental welfare or other assistance programs, involvement in crime and/or drugs, a solid foundation of education, etc.

Ask the following questions:

- What might today's pioneers be seeking, and what are the best routes to opportunity?

- If you had very little wealth, would it have been easier to make something of your life back in the 1830's, or would there be greater opportunities today?

Background

This problem-solving dilemma capitalizes on the overuse of southern land for the sole purpose of raising cotton. In particular, the virgin soil of Texas appealed to those southerners whose soil nutrients had been depleted.

Also borne out in this piece is the growing alarm with which the Mexican government began to view the hordes of American settlers of Texas. Once welcomed, they were an ever-increasing threat for Mexico. Of course, the fate of the independence of Texas would ultimately be determined by the famous armed insurrection led by men such as William Travis, Sam Houston, and Davy Crockett.

The Plight of the Pioneer

The Situation

You are a cotton planter living in Georgia in 1825. Since you have planted cotton year after year for almost twenty years, your soil is depleted. You have to sell your land in order to obtain money for land elsewhere and make a fresh start at what you know best.

You get little money for your worn-out Georgia land. It is barely enough to have your family start over in the Mexican-held territory of Texas where a living can be made relatively inexpensively. You and your wife, a twelve-year-old and an eighteen-year-old son, and a nine-year-old and twenty-year-old daughter make a difficult overland journey to Texas. While crossing the Mississippi River, your youngest son drowns. You lose half your possessions crossing the wild east Texas plains. However, you reach your destination of fertile land in east central Texas at last.

You pay a fellow American, Jim Smith, your remaining money for land — 200 acres of choice soil. During the first week there, Mexican officials ride into your camp and demand tribute (a tax) for settling on their land. If you do not pay within a month, you will be evicted. As you finish your house several weeks later, Comanche Indians ride in and order you off their land within two days.

Question to Consider

You have nothing to return to. What will you do?

Move Out!

Topic

Immigration to the United States, "The Trail of Tears" Indian removal of the 1830's

Objective

The students will practice problem-solving within a group setting. The students will compare their own contemporary values with the values of Americans in the past.

Materials

- page 63, reproduced (one copy per student)

Procedure

1. Group your students into teams of four.

2. Present the problem-solving dilemma to them.

3. Have the teams discuss their views on the situation for about ten minutes. During this time encourage teams to reread the dilemma together and state the issues in terms of the different points of view of the group members involved in the confrontation.

4. Have a designated spokesperson from each team share with the class the group's consensus (if it did reach one).

Background

This real-life situation has presented itself in the United States within the past decade. It is common when a new influx of immigrant labor threatens an established labor force. This problem-solving situation can be presented in context with several areas of immigration history. Most obvious is, of course, the great tide of immigrants — e.g., the Irish in the middle nineteenth century, the southern and eastern Europeans toward the end of that century, and the recent numbers of Hispanics and Asians arriving in the United States.

Move Out! *(cont.)*

Background *(cont.)*

Another saga of Americans can be very relevant to this activity.

The ''Trail of Tears'' was the forced removal of Native Americans from east of the Mississippi (notably the Cherokee) to Oklahoma and Kansas in the 1830's and 40's. This symbolizes what would be considered a modern injustice. However, it was done with little hesitation at the time in order to acquire more land to accommodate the white settlement.

Follow-Up

Offering this simulation before introducing the ''Trail of Tears'' may very well open students' minds to a metamorphosis in American thinking about cultural pluralism. A thought-provoking comparison/contrast could be made on ''The Trail of Tears'' removal issue by matching the prevailing rationale of the 1800's with the present viewpoints on civil rights. Encourage students to investigate the following questions:

* Could such an injustice occur today?

* Since so much is covered on television and radio news, not to mention magazines and newspapers, would it be impossible for such a thing to happen again?

* Are there any individuals or groups that specifically do not want immigrants (or any other minority group) to be part of America?

Cherokee Trail of Tears

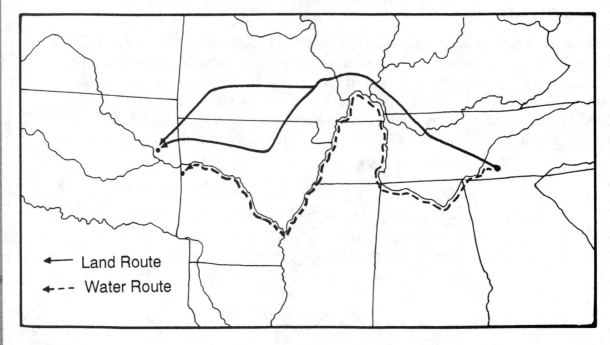

←— Land Route
←- - - Water Route

To Move or Not to Move

The Situation

In recent years, along a stretch of American coastal fishing areas, a new stream of immigrants has arrived hoping to continue their Old World trade. Many of these people have become citizens, but some remain as legal aliens.

With over-fishing and pollution causing a decreased supply of fish, many of the established fishermen resent this intrusion into their livelihood. They say that these newcomers are reducing an already shrinking fish population. Furthermore, as "red-blooded Americans," they feel that these "foreigners" do not have the right to infringe upon their life's work.

Some trouble has been reported. The new immigrants say they have been harassed and verbally threatened. Rumors have spread of physical violence toward the new fishermen and their families.

Questions to Consider

What do you think should be done?

Do the established American fishermen have sole right to the ocean's bounty?

Is there room for some new Americans to fulfill their dreams? What has happened in America in the past when situations like this (involving newly arrived immigrants) have occurred?

In your opinion, what would be the right thing to do?

Merchants and Miners

Topic

The California Gold Rush

Objectives

Students will use a variety of resources to compile pertinent data on the living conditions of the "forty-niners." Students will experience the economic principle of supply and demand.

Materials

- a variety of resources on the "forty-niners"— e.g., library books, reference materials, filmstrips, etc.

- pages 67 and 68, reproduced (as many as needed for the simulation)

Procedure

1. If students are not already in learning teams, set them up into groups of three of four. This should provide anywhere from five to nine groups in most classes.

2. Select one group to assume the role of the merchants near the California gold fields. The remaining groups will be miners, and all will be involved in a simulation dealing with the Gold Rush of 1849.

3. Students from all groups are to research the "forty-niners" specifically to identify what types of goods they would have needed to undertake life in the gold fields. Each group is to independently compile a list of items deemed mandatory for gold miners of this era. Each group's list will be known only to the group and to the teacher to whom they will furnish a copy. These groups will transact some business after their completed research. (See Procedure 5, page 65.) For the sake of the profit motive, any sort of collusion between groups would be counterproductive.

Merchants and Miners *(cont.)*

Procedure (cont.)

4. Of course, to have commerce, funds must be appropriated. In this case as students are using independent study time to research the "forty-niners," more than a week's time could be devoted to completing the rest of the chapter and/or unit on westward migration. (Students could also use a portion of each social studies lesson time for research, if the teacher so chooses.) Provide students with play money from pages 66 and 67. While answering group worksheet assignments, text questions, or in-class review questions, groups can be earning a dollar amount of Gold Rush money for each correct answer they provide in the week or so preceding their day of business. In this manner, a group could conceivably earn fifty to seventy-five dollars of Gold Rush money depending on the number of questions, activities, and correct responses given.

5. On the day the groups assume their roles, the merchant group "sets up shop," posting signs of their own design announcing their goods and prices. The merchants need to properly estimate how many of each item they should have on hand to be sure they have enough to supply the class needs. With a now-determined fixed amount of cash in hand, miners must peruse their lists to see how it matches the merchant's list and what they can afford. They may have to prioritize and buy only the most important item(s).

6. As previously mentioned, there is a profit motive beyond the use of play money. The money by itself means little to the students unless it can be exchanged for something more tangible. If your cooperative teams have been working towards a prescribed reinforcement, add to it with this activity. For every five dollars of goods sold by the merchant group, advance them one point or increment on that reinforcement schedule. The miners advance one point for every item that they purchase on their list. (Be sure the merchants hand out receipts.)

Merchants and Miners *(cont.)*

Background

"Merchants and Miners" is really two lessons in one. It presents the situation of the numerous miners, staking their lives and dreams out in the gold fields, being taken advantage of by the few merchants who were able to procure the needed supplies. A single egg would cost one dollar at a time that it could be had for a penny back East. Simultaneously, the students are learning a very basic economics lesson on supply and demand. It should become quite evident who is going to be getting the most reinforcer points as the merchant group makes sale after sale (provided they did adequate research).

Follow-Up

As a variation, on the next day have one miner group become a second merchant group and see what happens to the prices as supply begins to meet demand. You may wish to try this with three merchant groups. This reproduces what occurred historically as more and more miners began to realize a greater profit in abandoning their digs in order to service their former competitors.

Gold Rush Money

Gold Rush Money *(cont.)*

A Classroom Divided

Topic

The Civil War

Objective

The students will be motivated to learn more about the Civil War.

Materials

- a classroom social studies text and the usual materials employed by the teacher in addressing this unit

Procedure

1. To begin a unit on the Civil War, divide the members of the class into two teams representing the Union and the Confederacy. To approximate the ratio of northern states (23) to southern states (11) at the initiation of the conflict, two-thirds of your class should be on the North while the remaining one-third represents the South. Be sure to mentally divide your students into low, average, and high ability groups and give equal representation of each of these levels on both sides of the room as you assign the teams.

2. The sides should be physically distinct as well. Position desks so the two teams confront each other from across the room. Team members may draw maps of the particular state(s) they represent and display them alongside their desks. Allow this arrangement to remain each day for the duration of the unit. The number discrepancy not only represents the advantage the Union had in population but for purposes of this activity will also serve to illuminate the heavy favor it had in financial backing, industrial might and railroad networks.

3. Various cognitive tasks will make up the class ''war.'' Comprehension questions from the text, worksheet responses, map skill items, vocabulary, study sheet answers (among others) can serve as the basis for scoring points. Every item on every assignment (or designated assignments) will be the grounds for scoring points.

4. One point is awarded for each correct answer found on a team. For example, if a map worksheet pertaining to Civil War battles was assigned with five possible responses, and if there were fifteen Union students who all had perfect papers, those students would receive a total 75 points for the North. Conversely, on the same assignment, if all seven of the team members representing the South had perfect papers, they would score 35 points. The teacher can use as many opportunities (assignments) to score points as he/she wishes — the more assignments used, the greater the participation and interest of the students. Oral responses in reviewing previously-covered material may also be employed for points.

A Classroom Divided *(cont.)*

Procedure (cont.)

5. Keep track of the score on a daily basis and place the tally on a chart where all can view it. Obviously, with ability levels equally represented on both sides, the potential for collaboration on the assignments for "the good of the cause" is high. However, as long as the activities being used to gain points are practical in nature (and not evaluative), this form of "group assistance" is acceptable. The likelihood of the South "rising again" is also slim. This becomes obvious to the members of the Confederacy.

Follow-Up

While the numbers and scoring system purposely correspond to Union strengths entering the war, the Confederacy certainly had an advantage in leadership on the battlefield. To that end, you may wish to have several "battles" during the course of the unit. To be sure, they will be but intellectual jousts. Use a review game format such as college/quiz bowl or trivia games. You probably know of several other versions where the score obtained in the game is added to each team's collective point total.

The only catch in these review games is that each member must answer questions in sequence on his/her own. This gives the South an advantage in that its higher and middle ability levels will rotate faster than those of the larger North team. It gives the students of the "Confederacy" more motivation to succeed while also imitating the success the South enjoyed on the battlefield during the first half of the war.

"A Classroom Divided" is designed to keep students actively involved with the Civil War throughout the entire unit. Each teacher may determine whether or not there should be a reward at the end of the competition. The competition itself may provide enough motivation. For those concerned that the competitiveness may be too divisive, consider setting a class goal. Determine in advance what tasks you would like to include in your scoring system. Then set a class target based on the total score of both sides combined.

Set aside discussion time toward the end of the unit for the class to reflect on what enabled the Union to outlast the South. Discuss such questions as:

- What motivated the Confederacy to keep going?

- Were some of the respective advantages of each side exhibited in the class's competition? If so, how?

Sanctuary

Topic

The Underground Railroad

Objective

Students will offer a rational opinion (in oral and, perhaps, written form) about a hypothetical situation involving conscience versus the law.

Materials

- page 73, reproduced (one copy per student)

Procedure

1. Have the students prepared to work in groups of four.

2. Present each student with the dilemma on page 73. Orally read it with them.

3. Allow students time to think the problem over and then have them share with one person in the group their own sentiments about what they would do.

4. Ask the pairs in each group to share their thoughts with each other.

5. Finally, each group should combine with one other team in order to exchange various reactions to the scenario. (This step may be modified by having total class sharing if the teacher views it as preferable.) The three steps of sharing allow all students to express their viewpoints at least three times and to be exposed to at least six or seven potentially different opinions.

Sanctuary *(cont.)*

Background

While the names of the nations have been altered, you may recognize the real-life connotations involving Central American nations, such as El Salvador and Guatemala, and the United States. Even though this activity can certainly be used to study current Anglo/Latin-American relations, it can also offer dramatic relevance to younger students learning about abolitionists and the Underground Railroad in this nation during the last century.

In both situations students are faced with the dilemma of conscience versus the law. If you are utilizing this activity in conjunction with studies on the Underground Railroad, do not be too quick to draw a comparison between the two events. "A Question of Sanctuary" should be given several days before discussion begins on the Underground Railroad. This way students will hopefully offer a more genuine response to the dilemma of Maria without feeling prompted by the ideology of the abolitionists under study. Legitimate comparisons can be drawn between the way the American populace one hundred years ago could have been split over the workings of the conductors of the Underground Railroads and the dissention among members of your classroom over what to do about Maria.

Follow-Up

Along with a presentation that predates your Underground Railroad lesson(s), connect "Sanctuary" to Language Arts experiences as a critical thinking lesson. Have all students write their ideas about the dilemma, making sure to offer their reasoning for their viewpoints. Students should affirm whether their ideas were in any way influenced through the course of the groups' discussions.

A Question of Sanctuary

The Situation

Maria, a thirty-year-old mother, along with her two sons, Rodrigo (age 10) and Juan (age 8), have fled their native land of Augusto. They witnessed a killing of a neighbor who had spoken out against the government, and they now fear for their lives. Threats were made against them, and in other similar situations witnesses have also been harmed by marauding bands of thugs supportive of the government. Maria has taken her meager savings and her boys and has traveled almost one thousand miles into the land of Inde.

She is currently being housed by a church and its congregation. However, this is being done in secret because the government of Inde has a law that states that people from Augusto entering the country illegally will be deported to their homeland. Previous refugees from Augusto claimed that their lives would be in danger if they were forced to return. Officials in Inde usually deny these claims as wild stories and return the refugees anyway. Some of the returned refugees have been slain.

The members of this particular church, along with a network of several dozen more, believe people from Augusto like Maria and her family are in serious danger. Therefore, they go to great lengths to house, feed, and, in general, care for these people in hiding.

You are a citizen of Inde. You become involved when a friend of yours who attends this church confides in you as to what Maria's situation is after you see her ''sneak'' into the back of the church well after Sunday services were held.

Questions to Consider

What will be your response to your friend?

A law is being broken. What should you do? What will you do? Why? What consequences will your actions have for those other people involved?

Rockefeller

Topic

The rise of major industries (oil, steel, etc.) of the late nineteenth century

Objective

Students will attempt to be the first within a structured group to obtain a monopoly on a particular mineral commodity. Students will explain what a monopoly is.

Materials

- page 76, reproduced on index cards or heavy stock (one ''deck'' as prescribed in directions for every four-member group)

Procedure

1. Have the class grouped in teams of four. If you have an odd number, a group of five is preferred over a group of three.

2. One student in each group shuffles its deck thoroughly and deals out all the cards in the deck. In so doing, three members of a foursome will have twelve cards, and the fourth will have thirteen cards.

   No one may look at their hand until the dealer is ready to do likewise!

3. Once the dealer signals the go-ahead, cards may be traded by signalling for a particular number of cards only! Hand signals or oral commands may be honored provided the player sends all of one kind of commodity card in the transaction and that no mention of the commodity be made.

74

Rockefeller *(cont.)*

Procedure *(cont.)*

4. The "WILD" card comes into play in combination with seven of a particular commodity to form a winning hand. (Eight of a kind also wins.)

5. The first player to gain a monopoly of any kind shouts "Rockefeller!"

6. For extended play, tally points of the winning hands only. Usually one or two rounds is sufficient.

7. A basic strategy has the groups playing a practice hand followed by the initial scored round. If you wish, winners of the first round could meet head-to-head to determine the class's "Rockefeller" in an abbreviated tournament.

Background

It should be noted that "Rockefeller" is particularly active, and you may be hard pressed to maintain an appropriate noise level. Ideally, this simulation works best at the end of the day, especially on a Friday or any day preceding a vacation.

One effective way in which to study the rise of major industry and monopolies is by learning about the individuals who engineered and created those industries.

From his offices in Cleveland, John D. Rockefeller constructed a petroleum empire. For the most part, he was able to corner the market on oil in the latter stages of the nineteenth century and early portions of the twentieth. By buying up all the vital components needed to make the refinery business work (i.e., railroads, forests for lumber, barrels, ships, etc.) he created a monopoly. While "Rockefeller" may not lead any of your students down the road to riches, it is certain to impress upon them the zest with which individuals like Rockefeller pursued their goals. For the moment it will increase their adrenalin in hopes of defeating the competition.

Rockefeller Game Cards

See pages 74 and 75 for directions. Provide each group with a "deck" of cards consisting of eight each of "Coal," "Iron," "Copper," "Silver," "Oil," and "Gold." Reproduce one "WILD" card for each group.

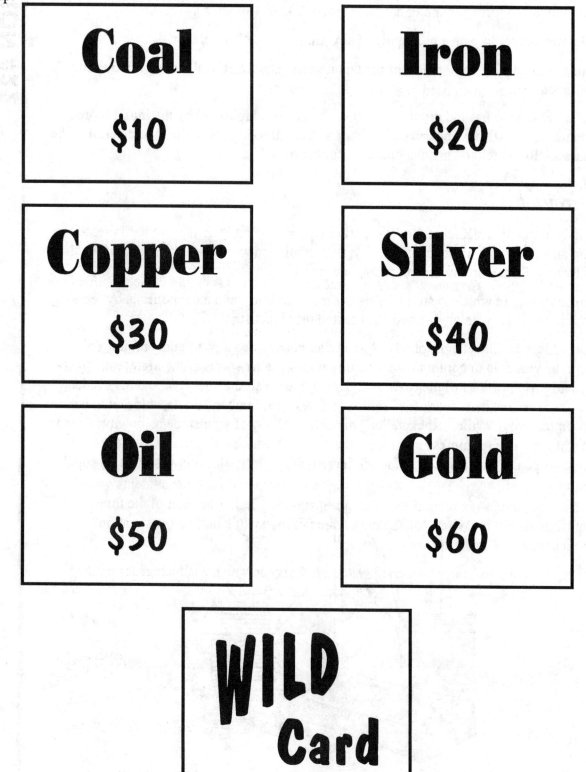

Coal $10	**Iron** $20
Copper $30	**Silver** $40
Oil $50	**Gold** $60

WILD Card

How the West Was Won

Topic

Indian wars of the Old West (1860-1890)

Objective

Students will identify one reason white settlers wanted Indian lands. Students will explain one method the government used in obtaining these lands.

Materials

- None

Procedure

1. The critical element in this activity is to place something valued by the entire class in jeopardy. While each teacher is in the best position to determine this factor, it is important to consider one which affects all the students and is highly valued by them.

2. Explain to the class that through negotiating with three class members, you have "purchased" the class's recess time in order to get some extra work done. The names will not be divulged, but they were paid off with some pens, pencils, and subject folders. (Forego the involvement of actual students due to the very stressful conditions to which they could be subjected.)

3. Observe class members' reactions toward the loss of recess and the way in which it was dealt away.

4. After a brief interlude of a minute or two, foster a class discussion regarding students' feelings about the lost recess. Ask the students why they think three students would sell recess time. Ask them if they thought it was their right (the right of the three students) to sell it. What would have been a fairer way of handling the situation? Which way was easier for me, the buyer?

5. After everyone has had a chance to vent their sentiments on the subject reassure the class that recess is not lost.

How The West Was Won *(cont.)*

Background

This activity is the anticipatory set for the study of the Indian Wars of the West. The United States government's standard procedure was to deal with less powerful individual Native American leaders while ignoring the majority of tribal members. From the colonial period on, whites had never fully appreciated the Indian's belief that land could not be owned since it was a gift from the Great Spirit. Native Americans despised the various treaties for these reasons. History had proven most of the treaties worthless anyway. The white man would take what was of value to him when the opportunity happened to arise.

The classic example of governmental procedure was exemplified with the Bozeman Trail debacle (1866-1868). To satisfy miners in Montana, the army tried to build a wagon road from Fort Laramie, Wyoming, into southern Montana. The problem was that it was blatantly placed across Sioux hunting grounds. The Sioux chieftain, Red Cloud, successfully waged a military campaign against the army which closed the trail. A treaty was signed, securing the Sioux their ancestral lands in the Black Hills of South Dakota. However, when gold was discovered there in 1874, miners paid no heed to words on paper as they were struck by ''gold fever.'' The ensuing conflict led to Custer's Last Stand and eventual capitulation of the plains tribes.

Follow-Up

This lesson veritably begs for a debate of some kind. Various cooperative learning groups could possibly take on the Native American side or the government's point of view. In lieu of a debate, the following question could be discussed within groups:

- ''How would our nation be different today if the American government had honored Native American treaties and not taken away their lands?''

 ©1993 Teacher Created Materials, Inc.

Jim Crow

Topic

Segregation in the post-reconstruction South

Objective

Students will define segregation and explain what "Jim Crow" laws did.

Materials

• For this simulation, design an activity sheet for the class in which each student responds to one of the problems/activities. Be sure that there are enough problems on the page so that each student will have a different problem to solve. Create the page so that the individual problems and activities can be cut out and distributed to each student. Create problems or activities with a variety of difficulty levels but keep in mind that they should be easy to correct. (For example, a math activity sheet might consist of division problems ranging from simple division to division of large numbers with fraction or decimal remainders.) You may create activity sheets on any concept from any discipline. Keep activities simple enough for students to respond to in approximately ten minutes.

Procedure

1. This activity provides an anticipatory set for a lesson on the onset of segregation laws in the South after Reconstruction.

2. Cut out the individual problems to allow for easy dispersal to the class.

3. A few minutes before you leave for a recess or lunch period (before your social studies lesson on segregation), give each student a problem to solve. Tell the class that you are going to start a new regimen for excusing them from class starting today. Distribute them at random or purposely give the hardest problems to select groups of students (e.g., those with glasses, blond hair, blue jeans, etc.). Do NOT delineate by race or ethnicity.

Jim Crow *(cont.)*

Procedure *(cont.)*

4. Instruct the students that in order to go to recess or lunch, each student must complete his/her problem. Some students stuck with the hardest problems will undoubtedly be a bit late. Accept a reasonable effort, especially if the student has limited ability with the problem. The objective will be to delay for recess or lunch certain students who have the most difficult problems to solve. The delay should be no more than five minutes and should not involve missing lunch or recess entirely.

For Discussion

After the class returns from lunch or recess, discuss with the class your "new procedure to release students." Elicit from students their feelings by asking them if this new procedure is or is not fair. Why or why not?

Lead into the segregation lesson by informing students that at some point in this nation's past, very difficult questions were used to determine if some people could vote. In fact, the most outrageously complicated questions were saved for one group of citizens to purposely (but legally) keep them from voting.

Background

By 1900, most southern states had been able to bypass the fifteenth amendment guaranteeing the African Americans' right to vote by incorporating a variety of legal devices designed to limit that vote. Known as "Jim Crow" laws, (named for an early 18th century white actor who wore black make-up in a minstrel show) they had various guises. Poll taxes (which discriminated against poor whites as well as blacks) and literacy tests were the two most prevalent means of denying African Americans the vote. Again, the literacy tests, while a legal requirement for all, were most stringently enforced against African Americans as they would have to read and explain complicated constitutional clauses and law. The segregation permeated not only the ballot but also how justice was doled out in court, seats on trains, water fountain use, etc. You may have recognized this activity as a spin-off from the old "brown eyes, blue eyes" theme. If you have not regularly used the simulations within this context throughout the year, "Jim Crow" will dramatically illustrate prejudice to your class.

Muckraker's Cake

Topic

Progressive reform of the early 1900's

Objectives

Students will identify who the Progressives were and recognize one industry they wanted regulated.

Materials

- two brownie cake mixes (and the ingredients listed on the box to prepare them)
- several long sticks of celery
- enough paper napkins for each student to have one

Procedure

1. For "Muckraker's Cake" to be most effective, you should have shared some edibles with your class throughout the year. Whether in the form of cookies, fruit, or pizza parties for rewarding outstanding work, a precedent is required. Without one, students may be very leery from the start and not fully involved in the simulation.

2. At home, prepare the two batches of brownie mix according to box directions with one notable exception. Add numerous fibrous veins from the celery sticks to the prepared mix. (Don't let the fibers become too wide. They should appear string-like.)

3. Create a reason to share a treat with the class such as a birthday celebration, reinforcement for some outstanding class work, celebrating Groundhog Day, etc.

4. As you begin to pass out the brownie treat, advise the students that you got a great bargain on the mix — an almost unbelievable price.

5. Enjoy the brownies and observe the students' reactions as they eat. Some will almost jump out of their seats when they discover the "stringy stuff," others will carefully note it and stop eating, and still others will notice nothing and continue to eat.

Muckraker's Cake (cont.)

Procedure (cont.)

6. As soon as the subject of ''stringy stuff'' is brought up, ask the following questions to determine what the substance could possibly be:

   • Do you think it is edible?

   • Take a close look at whatever it is.

   • If you do not feel safe eating it, throw the cake away.

   Observe how many students do throw their treat away rather than eat the foreign matter.

For Discussion

After everything is cleaned up, discuss the following questions with the class:

   • How many of you were in any way concerned about the nature of the material in the brownies?

   • Do you normally worry about having strange objects in your food? Do you know that a government agency protects us from tainted food? Have Americans always enjoyed such a standard of safety with our food?

Lead into a lesson about the Progressives and the reforms they wished to pursue.

Background

Employed by newly-formed monthly magazines at the turn of the twentieth century, the ''muckrakers'' were journalists who wrote exposés about many of society's ills. The articles about political corruption and industrial avarice were designed to gain readership. Before ''muckraking'' went out of style (due in large part to World War I), social reform also became an objective for some journalists.

Meat-packing was one of many industries exposed. Upton Sinclair's *The Jungle* uncovered the filth the immigrant employees worked in and the adulterated contents the public was actually consuming. One such incident found rope fibers used as filler in a meat product. Progressivism, a political philosophy of the era, espoused reform. Its proponents, including Teddy Roosevelt on many issues, wanted the government to regulate industries in order to protect the public. Many industries became government-regulated due to this movement.

Follow-Up

This activity could be used as part of a unit on health products, consumers, and the related regulatory governmental agencies.

A Woman's Place . . .

Topic

Women's suffrage movement (late nineteenth/early twentieth centuries)

Objective

Students will contrast the role of women in today's society with the role they played approximately a century ago.

Materials

- If you teach in a self-contained classroom, you may need a variety of repetitive drill worksheets dealing with basic mathematical computation. (Provide a copy of each drill for each girl in your class.)

Procedure

1. Start the day (or lesson) with an announcement that due to a United States Supreme Court ruling, certain changes will begin at school with respect to the girls in attendance. Since the court ruled women to be too fragile and tender for most physical work outside the home, female students will have to begin a regimen of limited physical activity at school. Recess time will be limited to the swings and nothing more exerting than a brisk walk. (If you could coordinate this announcement with your physical education instructor, it would have an even greater impact.) Running about and rowdy games will not be tolerated. Furthermore, it has been observed that females are not as adept in certain academic areas. Therefore, girls will adhere to straight drill work dealing with the basic facts in mathematics for the balance of the year. The presentation of other concepts would be viewed as a waste of time.

A Woman's Place . . . *(cont.)*

Procedure *(cont.)*

2. Ask the class if there is need for clarification on this new order. Use this opportunity to read the mood of the students, most notably the girls. If there is a strong negative reaction, elicit from the class specific reasons for their indignation. Have them counter the rationale of the Court's ruling with their own.

   This would be a good opportunity for students to get into cooperative discussion teams to share their feelings with other classmates. Classroom discussion would be preceded by the small groups' meetings. Time permitting, the discussions could be a basis for a written essay assignment — ''My View of the Supreme Court Ruling.''

3. If by some chance your class is apparently unmoved by the announcement, follow through with a close monitoring of the girls at the next recess (and a limited participation in that day's gym class). In the next math class provide repetitious drill work for the female students. (Those of you involved in a departmentalized setting would either have to work out an arrangement with the respective teacher(s) or prepare repetitious, monotonous tasks for the girls within your classroom.)

4. At any rate, when opposition toward the new code is voiced, allow for a structured response from the class, especially the girls. When they have responded with their oral or written views, explain such a Supreme Court ruling was indeed factual; however, it occurred in 1872! Do not allow the emotions created by this simulation to outlive the school day.

For Discussion

Proceed with the lessons on the women's movement of the latter nineteenth and early twentieth century that culminated with the nineteenth amendment in 1920.

Along the way, the contemporary women's movement should be discussed. Ask students to name new areas where women have entered previously male-dominated occupations. Discuss the following questions:

- In what ways has the role of women in today's society moved forward?

- In what areas do you think it lags behind the male role in society? Should there be specified male/female roles in a society?

Follow-Up

With the recent occurence of the Gulf War, students may recall women's roles in the military. In fact, as 1991 drew to a close, Congress authorized the use of female fighter pilots for the first time. Students may further debate the issue of what work there might be that should be strictly limited to one gender or the other. The question as to whether or not women should be used in combat military roles would be an interesting place to start.

84

Crash

Topic

Stock Market crash of 1929

Objective

Using material from the appropriate text, students will review the 1920's by simulating the meteoric rise of that decade's stock market that ended in the disastrous crash of "Black Friday," October 29, 1929. By participating in or observing the game, students should identify two reasons for the fall of the Stock Market.

Materials

- page 88, reproduced on index paper or heavy stock

- page 87, reproduced (one copy per student)

- pages 67 and 68, reproduced (Cut out denominations and provide $300 in play money for each student.)

- a pre-determined set of review questions relating to any current classroom study (to be used as game questions by the teacher)

Procedure

1. "Crash" is a unique game designed to review the 1920's era of American history. Students voluntarily enter into a game in which they can come up big winners or disappointed losers. First decide upon a realistic prize that you as the teacher are in a position to give and one the students deem worthy of pursuing.

2. In addition to a prize, choose an appropriate consequence such as a two-page report on a specific topic for anyone who becomes bankrupt in the contest.

3. These positive and negative consequences need to be incorporated in an official-looking contract. A contract is provided on page 87. The contract is meant to impress upon both parties that this is a valid, binding agreement.

Crash *(cont.)*

Procedure *(cont.)*

4. Each student in your class is to be apprised of the activity and the contract. While not all will risk a two-page report on such an academic undertaking, the more enticing the reward, the greater the chance that more students will go for it. After all, risk was all too great an element in the events leading up to the Stock Market Crash.

5. In "Crash," each participant begins with three hundred dollars in play money. If five or fewer students are competing, ten questions should be offered to each contestant in a specified number of rounds where the same question is presented to each contestant.

6. Contestants write their answers on a designated piece of paper and each player in turn shows his/her answer.

7. A correct answer is rewarded with one hundred dollars. An incorrect answer results in the drawing of the one of the "Penalty Events Cards" on page 88. These cards are indicative of the precarious financial situations in which many Americans found themselves by the end of the 1920's.

8. After ten questions (the ten rounds), any player to have reached one-thousand dollars is given the predetermined reward from his signed contract. Any player finishing with less than fifty dollars pays the fee (consequence) imposed by the contract.

Follow-Up

For more than five players, limit the questions to four or five rounds with correct answers scoring two hundred fifty dollars each. Penalties for incorrect answers remain the same. A student must be very knowledgeable to gain over one thousand dollars using this arrangement. Furthermore, a significant amount of luck is also entailed if one considers that only one incorrect answer out of ten (or out of four) could bankrupt a player. The "Black Friday" card ends the game for that particular player. After the "Penalty Event Cards" have all been used once, they are reshuffled and used again.

"Crash" is purposely designed for high-stakes risks (on an academic level) so students can, on their affective and cognitive levels, begin to relate to the financial disaster that many Americans faced in 1929.

Official "Crash" Contract

_____
(Student's Name)

voluntarily enters into this agreement with

_____
(Teacher/Guarantor)

on _____
(Date)

Whereas student scores a total of $1000 (one thousand dollars) he/she will

_____.

However, if said student retains less than $50 (fifty dollars) he/she will

_____.

Any potentially lucrative undertaking is beset with risks. I understand that the game "Crash" contains certain risks that may keep me from attaining $1000 or may even bankrupt me. I further realize that by answering all questions correctly I am immune to such risks.

_____
(Student's Signature)

Penalty Event Cards

Reproduce the following cards onto index paper, construction paper, or heavy stock. Laminate, if desired. Cut the cards out and place them face down on a playing surface for use with the simulation activity on pages 85-87.

Over-Invested in Real Estate

Lose one-fourth of your savings.

Factory Closed Due to Lack of Orders

Use up one-half of savings while looking for work.

Too Much Money Invested in Risky Stocks and Securities

Lose one-third of your savings.

Lose the Farm to the Bank

Lose three-fourths of your savings.

European Orders for Your Factory Dry Up in Europe's Depression

Lose one-half of your savings.

Your Interest on Mortgage, Car, and Personal Loans Excedes the Total Value of the Items

Lose one-half of your savings in payment toward interest.

October 29, 1929 Black Friday! You lose it all!

Does the Buck Stop Here?

Topic

The "Watergate" affair

Objective

Students will examine their personal values in regard to the behavior of public officials. Students will be introduced to the "Watergate" scandal.

Materials

- page 91, reproduced (one copy per student)

Procedure

1. Arrange students in cooperative learning teams.

2. Present the students with the problem solving situation on page 91 by orally sharing it with them.

3. Students in learning teams should deal with the activity before "Watergate" is ever introduced into class. The questions in the Follow-Up on page 90, are designed to encourage students to look at the ideal and/or pragmatically convenient responses that are plausible from the mayor's perspective.

For Discussion

Ask students to place themselves on the spot and express their values to the rest of the team. Every student should have the opportunity to share his/her thoughts within the team before the class as a whole reviews the problem.

After group and subsequent class discussion involving what the mayor should do (and what the students would do), ask the class if the mayor's role makes him/her more or less responsible in following the rules than, say, a governor or congressman or president.

Does the Buck Stop Here? *(cont.)*

Background

While various aspects of this problem-solving situation are different from the "Watergate" scandal, the basic premise remains constant.

Is any leader above the law in securing his/her office? Depending upon their life experiences, certain students will be more (or less) cynical than others. Previous wrongful acts by presidents and their appointed advisors (corruption in the Grant and Harding administrations comes to mind) can be used to lead into the "Watergate" affair. Affirm that this incident was not the first corrupt act by a president. However, its unraveling was complete enough to force the first resignation from the Oval Office in history.

Follow-Up

Discuss the following questions with the class:

- Does being President in charge of hundreds of governmental officials running an entire country make it harder to always know if your advisors are following the rules?

- Upon learning of illegal activities by one's staff, is the responsibility of the president any different from that of any other public official?

- Was the way the press investigated to uncover this scandal to be commended or criticized for interrupting the workings of the American federal government?

90

Re-Elect Mayor Jones?

The Situation

Mayor Jones of Ridgedale is in the middle of another re-election campaign. At age 61, he has been mayor of this city of 50,000 residents for the past twelve years. A former businessman, he sold his business thirteen years ago to run for mayor. Now his ambition is to get one more four-year term before he retires. Mayor Jones has been a good mayor for his city by many accounts. He has helped develop two new city parks, brought businesses back downtown, and was instrumental in getting a major highway project built around the southern outskirts of Ridgedale. While the highway project will make Ridgedale more attractive to business, it did cause many homeowners of that area to oppose it. They did not like the heavy truck traffic that would begin affecting their portion of the city. The election is less than two weeks away.

Mayor Jones now receives disturbing news from his attorney. His lawyer has discovered that George Little, the mayor's campaign chairman, has offered a $2,000 bribe to an outspoken neighborhood leader opposed to the highway project. Apparently, Mr. Little thought that he needed to quiet any serious opposition to the mayor in order to be sure of his re-election. Mayor Jones knows that Mr. Little's attempt at bribery was witnessed by no one. If the neighborhood leader did speak out about the attempted bribe, Mr. Little would deny it. It would simply be his word against the word of the other man.

Mayor Jones has a decision to make. He must either deny that he ever knew about any attempt at bribery by one of his officials, or he must openly admit to Mr. Little's crime and have the law discipline his good friend.

With less than two weeks to go before election day, the mayor's pollsters show him with a slight lead among potential voters.

Questions to Consider

What do you think the mayor should do?

What do you think he might do?

What are the possible consequences of his choices?

Which choice do you think is best for the city he serves?

What would you do if you were in the mayor's position?

Simulation Savvy Certificate

The spotlights are on

_____
(Student's Name)

for successfully participating
in American History team and individual
simulation activities.

_____
(Teacher's Signature)

_____
(Date)

92

Awards and Rewards

Several of the simulations in this book suggest the use of some type of acknowledgment in the form of a positive reinforcement for success or cooperative effort during the activities.

If a specific reward is not stated in the simulation activity, or if you do not wish to use the suggestions provided, try one of the alternatives listed below. This is a partial list of the awards and rewards you might decide to use.

Keep in mind that awards and rewards can fall into three major categories — recognition, privileges, and tangible rewards. No single kind of reinforcement works better than another. Select rewards for students depending on the grade level and/or the preferences of the students.

Privileges

- lunch with the teacher
- library pass
- computer use time
- pass for skipping homework
- peer tutor other students
- special ''helper'' for the day
- choice of some activity
- work on a special project, game, center, etc.

Recognition

- telephone call to parents
- name in class or school newspaper
- pat on the back for a job well done
- display work
- class cheer, chant, etc.
- student of the day, week, month
- note sent home to parents
- announcement to the class

Tangible Rewards

- popcorn party
- stickers
- bonus points or extra credit
- educational video or movie
- snack treats in the classroom
- grab bag or treasure chest
- hand stamp
- pencil, eraser, or other school supply
- tokens for no homework, extra recess, etc.

You may wish to use the map below as part of the extension tools for related cooperative team activities and simulations. Distribute copies to students as needed. Or prepare a transparency for use on the overhead projector.

United States Map

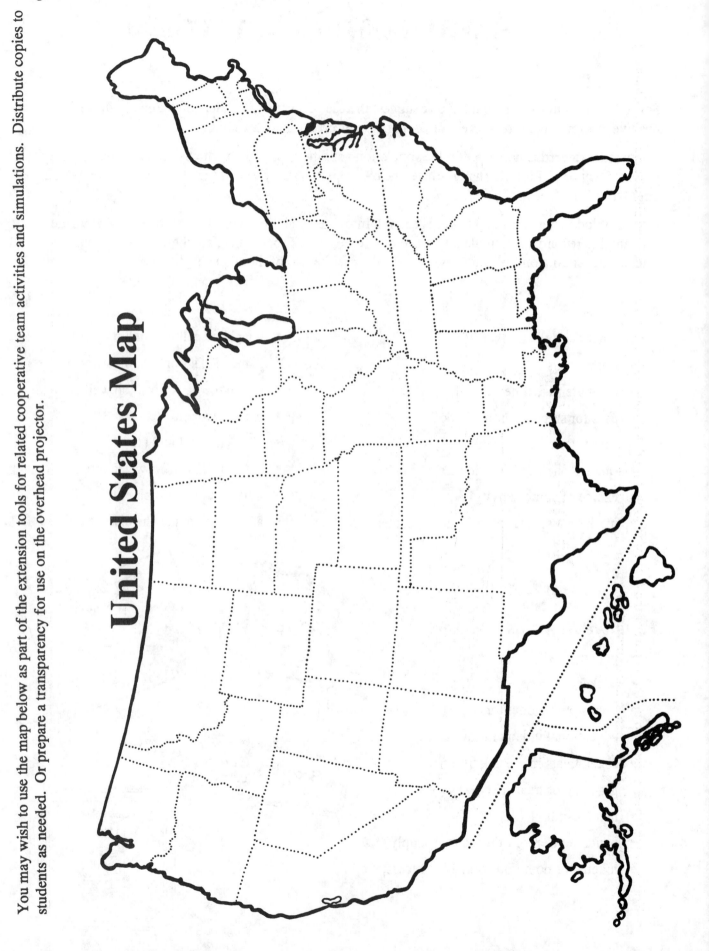

You may wish to use the map below as part of the extension tools for related cooperative team activities and simulations. Distribute copies to students as needed. Or prepare a transparency for use on the overhead projector.

World Map

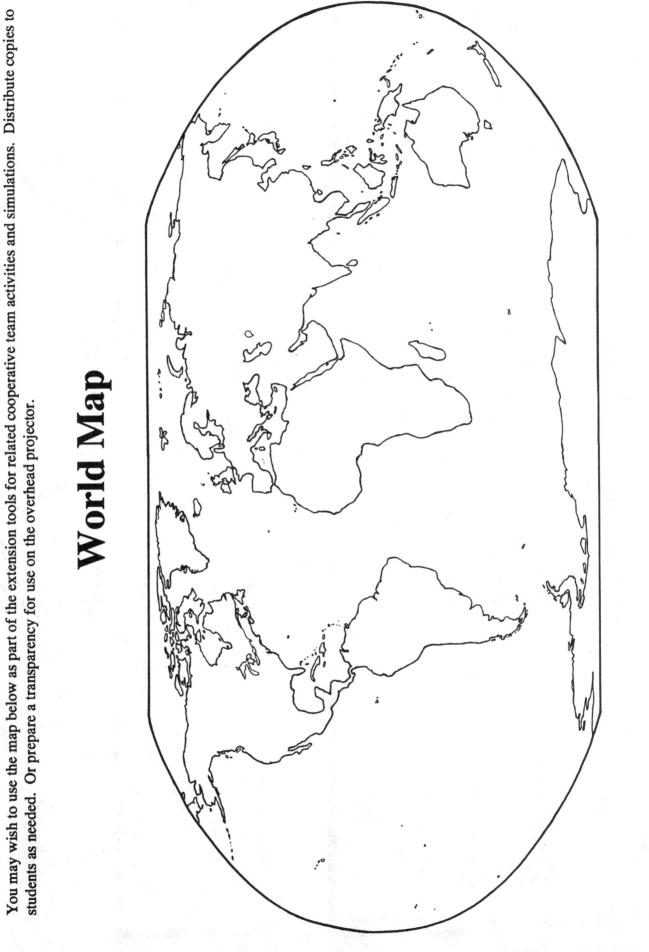

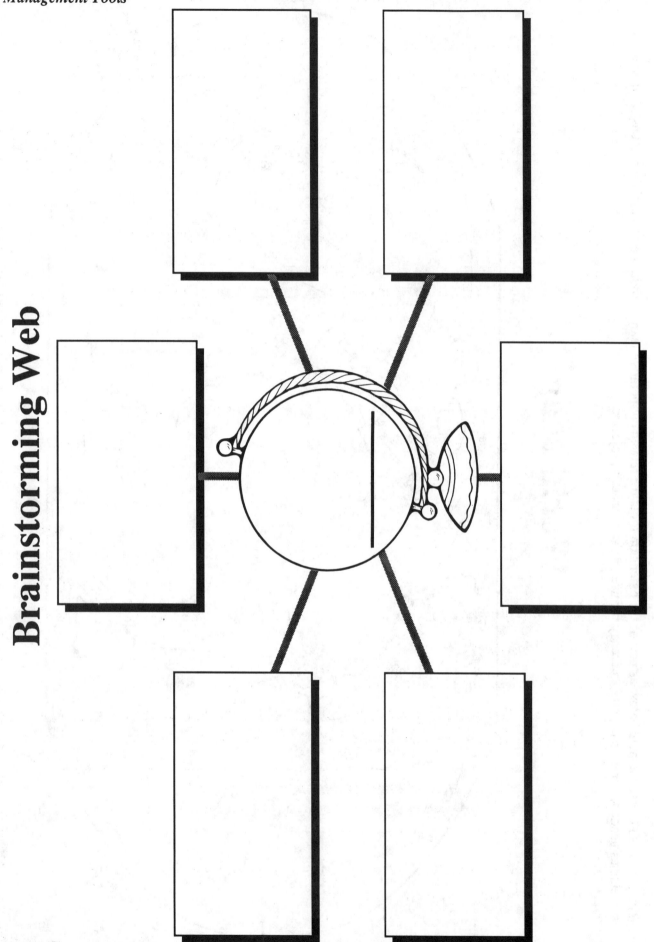

Brainstorming Web

96

THE ADVENTURES OF

Beekle

The Unimaginary Friend

★ THE ADVENTURES OF ★

BeeKLe

The Unimaginary Friend

Dan Santat

SCHOLASTIC INC.

He was born on an island far away where imaginary friends were created. Here, they lived and played, each eagerly waiting to be imagined by a real child.

Every night he stood under the stars, hoping for his turn to be picked by a child and given a special name.

He waited for many nights.

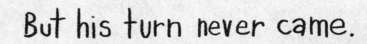

But his turn never came.

His mind filled with thoughts of all the amazing things that were keeping his friend from imagining him.

So rather than waiting...

...he did the unimaginable.

He sailed through unknown waters
and faced many scary things.

But thinking about his friend
gave him the courage to journey on...

...until he reached the real world.

The real world was a strange place.
No kids were eating cake.

No one stopped to hear the music.

And everyone needed naptime.

Then he finally saw something familiar....

So he followed.

He had a good feeling about this place.

But he looked everywhere,

and he could not find his friend.

He climbed to the top of a tree and looked out, wishing and hoping his friend would come.

But no one came.

He thought about how far he'd come and how long he'd waited, and felt very sad.

Then he heard a noise below.

 Hello!

Her face was friendly and familiar, and there was something about her that felt just right.

At first, they weren't sure what to do.

Neither of them had made a friend before.

But...

...after a little while

they realized

they were perfect together.

Beekle and Alice had many new adventures.

They shared their snacks. COLOR PENCILS

They told funny jokes.

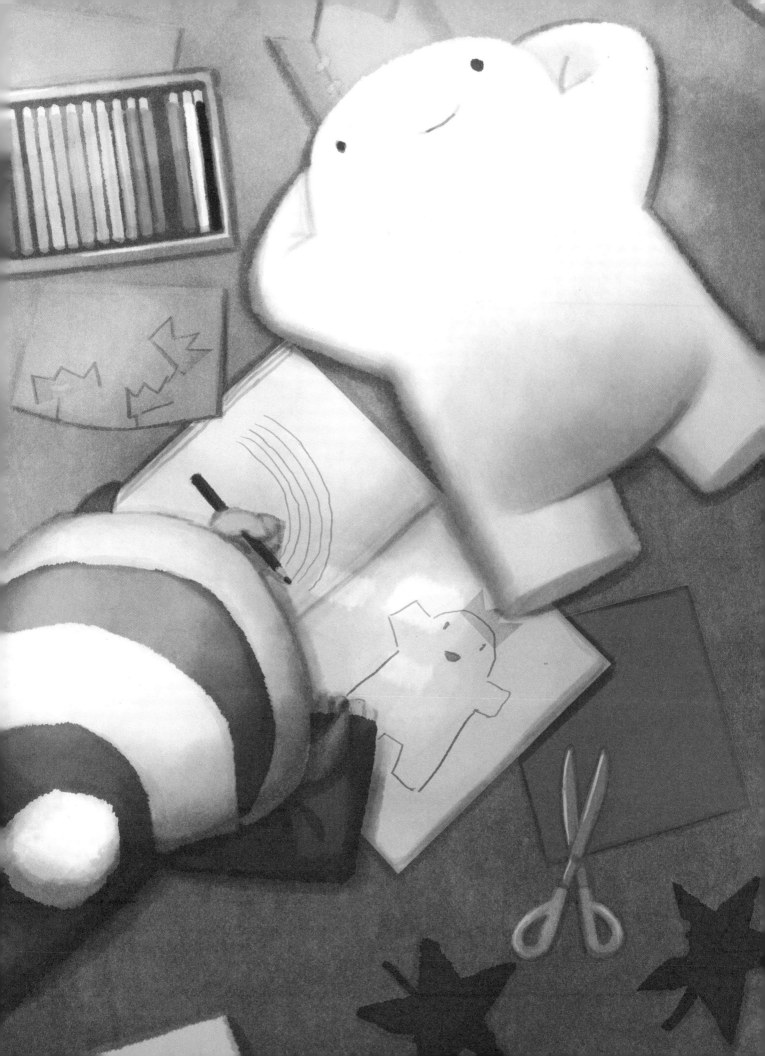

The world began to feel a little less strange.

And together they did the unimaginable.

-for Alek

ABOUT THIS BOOK:
This book was edited by Connie Hsu and designed by David Caplan.
The production was supervised by Erika Schwartz, and the production editor was Christine Ma.

The illustrations for this book were done in pencil, crayon, watercolor, ink, and Adobe Photoshop.
The text was hand-lettered.

ISBN 978-0-545-88091-6

12 11 10 9 8 7 6 5 4 3 2 1

15 16 17 18 19 20/0

Printed in the U.S.A.

This edition first printing, September 2015

David & Connie

"Beekle!"
—Alek, Age 1